"G. K. Chesterton once defined a paradox as 'truth standing on its head calling for attention.' And this, most certainly, is what Chris Castaldo achieves as he deftly guides us through the inverted glories of the Beatitudes in *The Upside Down Kingdom*. His beautifully written exposition invites these eight compressed theological H-bombs to graciously detonate within our hearts. *The Upside Down Kingdom* is not only a treasure trove of wisdom; it's also a bracing call to deeper devotion to Christ and the gospel."

R. Kent Hughes, Senior Pastor Emeritus, College Church, Wheaton, Illinois

"What happens if we read the Beatitudes from a relentlessly biblical perspective that interprets them in terms of the unmerited grace God has offered us in Christ? What happens when we read them in terms of what God has done *for* us in Christ's cross work, what he is doing *in* us by the Holy Spirit, and what he will do for the world *through* us? Chris Castaldo's *The Upside Down Kingdom* startles us with the answers. Here is a book that equips us to be the world's salt and light by helping us learn to live according to the 'rhythms of heaven' that beat in God's own heart."

Mark Talbot, Associate Professor of Philosophy, Wheaton College; author, Suffering and the Christian Life series

"To modern readers, the Beatitudes can sometimes sound confusing or even off-putting. Chris Castaldo does a lovely job demystifying Jesus's teachings—and therefore making them truly beautiful—for Christians today. His explanations and examples are easy to grasp, giving context in a gentle and winsome way. This book would be perfect for a group Bible study or individual devotions—I read with my Bible on my lap, highlighting and making notes the whole way through."

Sarah Zylstra, Senior Writer, The Gospel Coalition; coauthor, *Gospelbound: Living with Resolute Hope in an Anxious Age*

"I love this book. Thank you, Chris Castaldo, for the gift of *The Upside Down Kingdom*. This warm, engaging, and yet thought-provoking work wonderfully draws us to the vision of the Beatitudes. In the words of Castaldo, this is 'a vision that invites us from the shadows of alienation into the purpose and joy of Christ's kingdom.' Truly, when we embrace this counterintuitive vision and way of life, we will be portraits to a watching world of what it looks like to live according to God's heart."

Crawford W. Loritts, Jr., author; speaker; radio host; President, Beyond Our Generation

T0028315

"Chris Castaldo is a model pastor-theologian, and *The Upside Down Kingdom* puts his considerable pastoral and theological gifts on full display. Wise and winsome, subtle and profound, thought-provoking and heart-warming, his exposition of the Beatitudes captures the living voice of their original author and thus provides a tonic for the lackadaisical and a solace for the beleaguered—an invitation into Jesus's upside-down kingdom. Beautifully done! Highly recommended!"

Todd Wilson, Cofounder and President, Center for Pastor Theologians

"Chris Castaldo has issued a timely and desperately needed prophetic call for the church to embody the lordship of Jesus Christ in distinctly countercultural and counterintuitive ways within our increasingly polarized world. Incorporating depth of biblical-theological reflection, historical perspective, pastoral experience, and cultural sensitivity, with appropriate nuance and refreshing personal honesty, this book warmly invites us to experience the blessedness of identity in Christ as we align our affections and allegiances more fully with Christ and his kingdom. In a day of significant cultural confusion, *The Upside Down Kingdom* is a clarion call for Christian identity and ethic."

Laurie L. Norris, Professor of Bible, Moody Theological Seminary; coeditor, *One Volume Seminary: A Complete Ministry Education from the Faculty of Moody Bible Institute and Moody Theological Seminary*

"The Beatitudes are a special part of the New Testament. Chris Castaldo's excellent exposition brings them to life with the aid of real-life examples and the wisdom of the ages. A challenging and inspiring book that is recommended to all."

Tony Lane, Professor of Historical Theology, London School of Theology

"I've learned a lot from Chris's teaching and example of following Christ through the counterintuitive turn of the kingdom. And I'm thrilled that many more will benefit likewise with this book. When we realize the way up first goes down, then we'll find the power of God to overcome today's challenges."

Collin Hansen, Vice President and Editor in Chief, The Gospel Coalition; author, *Timothy Keller: His Spiritual and Intellectual Formation*

The Upside Down Kingdom

The Upside Down Kingdom

Wisdom for Life from the Beatitudes

Chris Castaldo

 CROSSWAY®

WHEATON, ILLINOIS

Library of Congress Cataloging-in-Publication Data

Names: Castaldo, Chris, 1971- author.
Title: The upside down kingdom : wisdom for life from the beatitudes / Chris Castaldo.
Description: Wheaton, Illinois : Crossway, [2023] | Includes bibliographical references and index.
Identifiers: LCCN 2022041836 (print) | LCCN 2022041837 (ebook) | ISBN 9781433584916 (Trade paperback) | ISBN 9781433584923 (PDF) | ISBN 9781433584947 (ePub)
Subjects: LCSH: Beatitudes. | Christian life–Study and teaching.
Classification: LCC BT382 .C385 2023 (print) | LCC BT382 (ebook) | DDC 226.9/3--dc23/eng/20221123
LC record available at https://lccn.loc.gov/2022041836
LC ebook record available at https://lccn.loc.gov/2022041837

---

*This book is dedicated with love
to Luke, Philip, Simeon, Aliza, and Malachi*

Contents

Acknowledgments

I AM GRATEFUL FOR FRIENDS whose encouragement motivated me to embark on this project, namely R. Kent Hughes, Collin Hansen, Terri Hands, and my colleagues at the Center for Pastor Theologians.

I am also thankful for several friends who have kindly read this book in draft and have offered suggestions, corrections, and clarifications. They are not responsible for any weaknesses that remain. I think particularly of Stan Guthrie, Carolyn Thayer, John Neuenkirchen, Bruce Callender, Karyn Hecht, Doug O'Donnell, Mike McDuffee, Bryan Litfin, Joel Lawrence, Kristin Neva, Allyson Brown, and Tony Balsamo.

Heartfelt thanks to Bishop Julian Dobbs and the Anglican Diocese of the Living Word with whom I had the privilege of first sharing this material at their 2021 clergy and spouse retreat.

To New Covenant Church in Naperville, whose hunger and thirst for righteousness is an inspiration and ongoing gift, thank you for the privilege of letting me serve as your pastor.

I want to acknowledge Todd Augustine and Justin Taylor, whose enthusiasm and expertise brought the manuscript to the light of day.

Finally, I thank God for my dear wife, Angela, and our five amazing children—Luke, Philip, Simeon, Aliza, and Malachi—to whom this book is dedicated. Your sacrifice has made it possible.

For theirs is the kingdom of heaven

MATTHEW 5:3

Introduction

You Are Invited

WHEN WE PRAY for God's kingdom to come "on earth as it is in heaven" (Matt. 6:10), we sometimes imagine the kingdom to be far away. It is, however, closer than we think. In the crucified and risen King, the two realms now overlap—a holy ground that is simultaneously mundane and heavenly, temporal and eternal.

Jesus's Beatitudes are concerned with cultivating this kingdom life, though perhaps not in the way we would expect. For many, the Beatitudes are thought to increase our happiness by imparting blessings—at least that's the impression our Israeli tour guide gave us. Facing the shimmering Sea of Galilee, she portrayed the rabbi from Nazareth on a grassy slope, holding forth in a flowing violet robe, encircled by attentive disciples. "Here, Jesus offered the secrets to living a happy life," she explained.[1]

Unfortunately, the gently blended lines of this portrait easily obscure the stark, counterintuitive thrust of Christ's kingdom. Our guide's pastel-colored depiction may offer comfort, but it's not where we live. Many of us labor under nagging concern for our children, encroaching loneliness, financial disaster, and creeping old age. We are haunted by the past and afraid of the future. We are troubled over the brokenness in our communities. Scammers prey on the elderly and walk away laughing. Victims of abuse wrestle with heartache and bitterness. In our world, naked with lust and greed, people often grab whatever they can get. And just when we start to feel morally superior to those wretches "out there," we find uncomfortable traces of this evil in ourselves. Aleksandr Solzhenitsyn bluntly observed, "The line dividing good and evil cuts through the heart of every human being."[2]

In this familiar cauldron of life and death, of struggle and strain, how does one experience the peace of God's kingdom? The Hebrew word for peace is of course "shalom." It describes life as God intended, the long-awaited age in which his manifest glory would set the world right, making crooked places straight and rough places smooth. Weeping would become joy, mountains would drip with fresh wine, and deserts would flourish with life. In the words of Cornelius Plantinga Jr.,

> People would work in peace and work to fruitful effect. Lambs could lie down with lions. All nature would be fruitful, benign, and filled with wonder upon wonder; all humans would be knit together in brotherhood and sisterhood; and all nature and all humans would look to God, walk with God, lean toward God, and delight in God.[3]

This is the vision of the Beatitudes—a vision that invites us from the shadows of alienation into the purpose and joy of Christ's kingdom. But, as we shall see, this blessedness is both counterintuitive and countercultural.[4] The Beatitudes pour gasoline on our contemporary ideals—and then light a match. To satisfy our hunger for wealth, Jesus offers poverty. He extols meekness over hostility. Rather than personal pleasure and fame, he proposes patience and a commitment to justice. Instead of lust and greed, he commends purity of heart. For the soul riddled with anxiety and fear, he offers peace. Rather than vanity and pride, he bestows security and inner strength. The Beatitudes dig beneath the surface, exposing what we really need to value and practice. Servais Pinckaers suggests that we can compare the work of the Beatitudes to that of a plow in the fields. "Drawn along with determination," he writes, "it drives the sharp edge of the plowshare into the earth and carves out, as the poets say, a deep wound, a broad furrow."[5] This blessed furrow uproots the weeds of our pride and perversion, renewing the soil of our souls, a renewal in which the eternal fruit of God's kingdom burgeons with life.

By excavating the attachments of our soul, the Beatitudes reveal the pernicious lies we have internalized while simultaneously portraying the life God intends for his people. In them Jesus is not, as many suppose, offering a religious ladder can be climbed all the way up to a smiling Deity who rewards our religious effort. Nor is he giving an ideal moral system reserved for an elite group of chosen disciples, or laying out a penitential program whereby one receives divine blessing by assuming the posture of a doormat.

Rather, Jesus is describing the man or woman who belongs to his Father's kingdom and therefore lives according to God's heart. These blessed ones lived in the "shadow of death," but now "a light has dawned" (Matt. 4:16), a divine illumination that offers a new logic. In this fallen world, it's the wealthy, the charming, and the strong who are exalted. But Jesus shows us that God's heart—full of steadfast love and faithfulness—extends to the weak, the vulnerable, and the awkward. Throughout his parables, Jesus makes the marginalized and oppressed the heroes, an ironic and unexpected turn that explodes like fireworks throughout his teaching. He preached:

> Blessed are the poor in spirit, for theirs is the kingdom of heaven.
> Blessed are those who mourn, for they shall be comforted.
> Blessed are the meek, for they shall inherit the earth.
> Blessed are those who hunger and thirst for righteousness, for they shall be satisfied.
> Blessed are the merciful, for they shall receive mercy.
> Blessed are the pure in heart, for they shall see God.
> Blessed are the peacemakers, for they shall be called sons of God.
> Blessed are those who are persecuted for righteousness' sake, for theirs is the kingdom of heaven.
> Blessed are you when others revile you and persecute you and utter all kinds of evil against you falsely on my account. Rejoice and be glad, for your reward is great in heaven, for so they persecuted the prophets who were before you. (Matt. 5:3–12)[6]

Our Counterintuitive Calling

The Greek word rendered "blessed" (*makarios*) is rich in meaning. There is no single term in English that conveys its complexity, beauty, and nuance.[7] Some suggest the word "fortunate" best conveys the idea because it describes a valuable gift that cannot be earned.[8] Others have translated *makarios* as "happy." Augustine, for example, takes this approach, identifying happiness as the goal and outcome of a righteous life, a gift that one enjoys in communion with Christ.[9] But however sure the link between happiness and holiness, this understanding must be supplemented by the full-orbed, biblical conception of blessedness offered to us in the Beatitudes.

The fleeting nature of worldly happiness, after all, is not sturdy enough to sustain the eternal weight of glory to which Jesus points us. "Happiness," wrote William Bennett, "is like a cat. If you try to coax it or call it, it will avoid you: it will never come."[10] Nevertheless, it's still commonplace to hear Christians promoting "Be-Happy Attitudes," as Robert Schuller used to say.[11] In his book by that title, Schuller offers motivational insights to fortify the church with cheerfulness. For instance, he paraphrases the blessing upon mourners with the affirmation, "I'm really hurting—but I'm going to bounce back!"[12] The message of positive thinking is clear: the right attitude and sufficient effort will produce the happiness we desire.

Life in the kingdom, though, is not about striving for happiness or avoiding the ills of human existence. It's about *receiving* and *finding*. It's about recognizing and living into God's promises, even amid the pain and suffering of life (Eph. 1:3; James 1:17). "Blessed" is therefore not an achievement, attitude, or a subjective emotion; it is the tangible gift of God's loving embrace, an identity in Christ that experiences life as it *ought* to be—"as in heaven."

God's blessing, however, goes even further. In addition to saving our own souls, the Beatitudes set forth the clearly demarcated way of righteousness in the world. Thus, when Dietrich Bonhoeffer (1906–1945) started a seminary for the Confessing Church at

Finkenwalde, it was modeled on the Sermon on the Mount.[13] Fiercely opposed to Hitler, Bonhoeffer and his colleagues employed the Beatitudes to confront the Nazi's devilish propaganda and influence. Here is how Craig Slane explains it:

> Bonhoeffer believed that it was possible for a community gathered on the basis of Jesus' Sermon on the Mount to provide the necessary ground for resistance against tyranny. The practices of dying to one's self in confession, meditation, and intercession produced openness to others and forged the kind of solidarity required for moral risk-taking.[14]

Like Bonhoeffer, we must put Jesus's message into the foreground. We must stress, as he did, that the only place on earth where one finds this beatitudinal life "is where the poorest, meekest, and most sorely tried of all men is to be found—on the cross at Golgotha."[15] The wealthy, charming, and strong, as it turns out, may become the greatest tragedies of all because they rely on their natural gifts. But people who lack such advantages, or those who are courageous enough to confess their need for God, are poised to receive his blessing.

The Beatitudes, therefore, answer the essential questions of identity and calling by placing squarely before us a counterintuitive kingdom that inexorably aligns our affections and priorities with the rhythms of heaven. Here we find the "blessed" life that God intends for his people—not just in the future, but here and now.

We begin by considering the "poor in spirit, for theirs is the kingdom of heaven" (Matt. 5:3).

The Poverty That Makes One Rich

Blessed are the poor in spirit,
for theirs is the kingdom of heaven.

MATTHEW 5:3

MIKE VETRONE was accustomed to luxury sports cars and beachside mansions during his years as a drug runner for the New York Mafia, a lifestyle that is now a distant memory. "With judges, court clerks, and casino officers on the payroll, I pranced through Atlantic City like the mayor," he says now.[1]

Yet Mike soon began a descent into a heroin addiction that threatened his life. After a customer discovered that Mike had stolen some of his drugs, Mike packed a bag and fled to Florida. Menacing death threats followed him, intimidation that continued for months. "I remained alone," he remembers, "bound by my addiction, facing a dismal future."

He began thinking of suicide. "I was now haunted by what was, in fact, a not altogether unpleasant idea of ending my misery with the click of a trigger," Mike says. "My .22 caliber handgun, which was usually within arm's reach, held a fresh cartridge. After two years, the moment of reckoning had come."

On an uncharacteristically overcast morning in South Florida, Mike dropped by a favorite haunt, Big Apple Bagel, to pick up what he assumed would be his last meal. Back in his apartment, he flipped on the television, looking for company one last time as he ate. On came a television preacher. With a distinct southern accent, the man exclaimed, "Life has a way of grabbing you by the collar, forcing you down to your knees."

Mike turned up the volume.

"There's a chain that binds every soul," the preacher exclaimed, "and that chain is sin—an addiction from which Jesus's death and resurrection sets us free." Suddenly, as the television evangelist invited viewers to embrace Christ, Mike felt energy pulsing through his veins and found himself shouting at the television, "Yes!" In that moment, he no longer felt alone but sensed an encircling presence. Mike was facing not the end of his life, but a new beginning.

I met Mike in 1995 while serving as a pastoral intern in South Florida. For nearly three months, I shadowed him, learning that the addicted, downtrodden, and hopeless are the people who are poised to receive the blessing of God. The kingdom, I learned from Mike, is not for the graspers, but for the broken—those who reach the end of themselves and approach God with empty hands. Such people recognize that "they are completely and utterly destitute in the realm of the spirit."[2]

This is what it means to be "poor in spirit" (Matt. 5:3). Unlike the Pharisees of Jesus's day—full of religious swagger—the spiritually poor see their bankruptcy. They know that they can do nothing to merit divine favor. So, they depend on the Lord's provision, the one who gives the most magnificent gift imaginable—himself.[3] Indeed, this living relationship with the King defines what it means to participate in the kingdom, not in the far-off future, but right now. Today.

The Dominion of Dependence

Impoverished spirits have a long ancestry. Hearing God's promise to make of him a great nation and to bless the world, Abraham "obeyed" and "went," leaving the wealth and security of his home (Heb. 11:8). Through shimmering mirages, he wandered through deserts and into cities, trusting the one who had called him. A mortified and empty Jacob faithfully wrestled with God and exclaimed, "I will not let you go unless you bless me" (Gen. 32:26). And a jailed Joseph trusted God in Egypt (Gen. 39–41). In countless ways, Israel experienced poverty.

After four hundred years of silence, God's people continued to anticipate the long-awaited kingdom. Matthew's Gospel, where we find the Beatitudes,[4] sets the stage in its opening chapters. Like the nation of Israel, Jesus travels down to Egypt, meets a hostile king, returns from Egypt, passes through the water, and enters the wilderness. In these movements, Matthew portrays familiar turns of salvation history, but with a twist.

This portrait features Christ as the realization of Israel's destiny, the long-anticipated King of the kingdom (Matt. 16:28; Luke 17:21). Time collapses as Jesus enters the stage of history as the ultimate servant and faithful offspring of Abraham who fulfills God's promise (Gal. 3:16–18; 2 Cor. 1:20). Matthew is rhetorically shouting to his readers that Jesus is the culmination of Jewish hope. He records, "From that time Jesus began to preach, saying, 'Repent, for the kingdom of heaven is at hand'" (Matt. 4:17).

The phrase "kingdom of heaven" occurs throughout Matthew and is generally synonymous with "kingdom of God."[5] It describes the true, peaceful, pure, and joyful life that is realized in communion with God (see Matt. 4:23). Such blessings confront our idols—the gods of comfort, success, and national pride—and promise something far greater.[6] Indeed, idols are merely the profane and twisted parody of which the kingdom is the satisfying reality. So, Jesus frames his Beatitudes with reference to the kingdom: "Blessed are the poor in spirit, for theirs is the kingdom of heaven" (Matt. 5:3; see 5:10).

Notice how Jesus describes the kingdom of heaven as "theirs." The positioning of this word at the beginning of the clause gives the sense that the kingdom is for this particular group, the poor in spirit, the marginalized and forgotten—and not for the rich, self-assured, ambitious, or proud. It's not for those who are content with life and consistently in control. It's not for those who believe in themselves, who have the natural ability to win the day. As Martin Luther proclaimed from his deathbed, "We are all beggars; this is true."[7]

In his 1520 treatise *The Freedom of a Christian*, Luther makes this point by describing a king who marries a prostitute, which results in the sudden change of her identity. She is now the queen, acquiring all the privileges associated therein. In one sense, of course, she remains the very same person. When she looks in the mirror, she sees the same old face staring back at her. And yet now, because of the king's love, her status has radically changed. Having heard his wedding pledge, "You are my beloved and I am yours," the queen is secure (see Song 2:16).

In like manner, says Luther, Christ, the bridegroom, takes our sin as his own. Luther writes,

> Who can even begin to appreciate this royal marriage? What can comprehend the riches of this glorious grace? Here, this rich, upstanding bridegroom, Christ, marries this poor, disloyal little prostitute, redeems her from all her evil and adorns her with all his goodness. For now it is impossible for her sins to destroy her, because they have been laid upon Christ and devoured by him. In Christ, her bridegroom, she has her righteousness, which she can enjoy as her very own property.[8]

This, according to Luther, is the "great exchange" in which all that the church has (her sin) is given to the King and all that he has (justice, blessedness, life, and glory) is bestowed on her. Condemnation is therefore now in the past, as Luther exclaims: "Believe in Christ, in whom grace, righteousness, peace, freedom, and all things are promised to you. If you believe, you will have these things; if you do not believe, you will lack them."[9]

Here is where it gets especially practical. Each day when we look into the mirror, we face a shameful sinner who falls short of moral beauty and excellence. Embarrassed by this honest estimation of ourselves, we groan, "How long, O LORD?" (Ps. 13:1). We descend into the valley of self-loathing and despair. But then, just as our souls enter this familiar and dreaded valley, we remember the King's vow, his promise that lifts us from our downward spiral: "In my Father's house are many rooms. If it were not so, would I have told you that I go to prepare a place for you? And if I go and prepare a place for you, I will come again and will take you to myself, that where I am you may be also" (John 14:2–3).

Billy Graham wisely said, "When we come to the end of ourselves, we come to the beginning of God."[10] In God's kingdom, the valley is the turning point. If you've ever read a Dostoyevsky novel, you've seen variations of this theme. Some smart and influential figure is battered and bruised by the failures and defeats of life until he crawls into a fetal position and pleads for mercy. That's the necessary inflection point where the direction of life changes.

The high and mighty are not able to hear this word. Only the lowly hear it. So the Lord says, "This is the one to whom I will look: he who is humble and contrite in spirit and trembles at my word" (Isa. 66:2). This was Isaiah's point when he declared that only the remnant of believers would remain in the land (Isa. 6:12–13) and that they would depend not on themselves, but on the promise of God (Isa. 10:20–23). Zephaniah hits the same note:

> But I will leave within you
>   the meek and humble.
> The remnant of Israel
>   will trust in the name of the Lord. (Zeph. 3:12 NIV)

This is the spirit Jesus describes in the Beatitudes, of those who have been emptied and are now ready to be saved. It was the spirit of the eighty-year-old Moses at Mount Horeb before the burning bush, sufficiently emptied of his savior complex and ready to listen. It was the spirit of Jeremiah, whom God had called:

Before I formed you in the womb I knew you,
and before you were born I consecrated you;
I appointed you a prophet to the nations. (Jer. 1:5)

Before Jeremiah's initial breath—indeed, before his conception—God determined to speak through his weakness and poverty, and this grace would illustrate God's character through the
centuries. We can also look at the austere obedience of John the
Baptist or the repeated sufferings of the apostle Paul, the one to
whom God said, "My grace is sufficient for you" (2 Cor. 12:9).
Most importantly, there is the supreme example of our Lord Jesus
Christ, God's suffering servant:

He grew up before him like a tender shoot,
    and like a root out of dry ground.
He had no beauty or majesty to attract us to him,
    nothing in his appearance that we should desire him.
He was despised and rejected by mankind,
    a man of suffering, and familiar with pain.
Like one from whom people hide their faces
    he was despised, and we held him in low esteem.
        (Isa. 53:2–3 NIV)

The Contours of Human Poverty

Poverty often comes uninvited. Sometimes it is thrust upon us.
The poor and disenfranchised—in their need for food, clothing, housing, and employment—know this reality. Illness is
another form of poverty, especially when chronic pain is part of

the picture. We experience poverty of affection—the paucity of a parent's love that stunts a child's growth, a spouse who withdraws relationally, or the isolation that sometimes accompanies singleness. Advanced years can become a poverty as strength fails and abilities diminish. This is certainly true for those with Alzheimer's as well as their family members. All of this poverty is at some level interconnected and leads to the ultimate experience of poverty—the primal hardship called death.

Yet Christ doesn't leave us to languish and die in this condition. He fully embraced our impoverishment, being born in a manger and having nowhere to lay his head. By such humility, Jesus assumed human frailty and deprivation, a condescension that led redeemed humanity through the darkness of the cross into the radiance of eternal life. In the words of Paul, "For you know the grace of our Lord Jesus Christ, that though he was rich, yet for your sake he became poor, so that you by his poverty might become rich" (2 Cor. 8:9).

This is where the poor in spirit go—to the cross of Christ—for there our desperate plight is revealed. There, at the cross, we are exposed as inadequate in a world that values winners. There we are left naked and discovered to be cursed by the Judge whose verdict matters forever. But then we discover the good news: that on the cross Jesus died in our place, shedding his blood to purge our sin. In this encounter, says Jonathan Edwards, repentant sinners "unexpectedly find him with open arms to embrace them, ready forever to forget all their sins as though they had never been. They find that he runs to meet them, and makes them most welcome, and admits them not only to be his servants but his friends."[11] Again, in the words of our beatitude, "Blessed are the poor in spirit, for theirs is the kingdom of heaven" (Matt. 5:3).

To be clear, this poverty is not an impulsive plunge into destitution or a masochistic disregard of responsibility in favor of pain or failure. Neither is it the cloistered asceticism of hermits. It is, rather, a humble and honest recognition of our spiritual bankruptcy. As the Psalmist put it, "If you, O LORD, should mark iniquities, O Lord, who could stand?" (Ps. 130:3).

Such poverty of spirit, says the Puritan preacher Robert Harris (1581–1658), is the starting point of life—the realization of one's "extreme need" of salvation: "Thus God undoes a man before He saves him, mars him before He makes him, takes him all to pieces and then joins him together forever."[12] Such transformation occurs in the daily rhythms of life—before God, in our communities, and in the church. We'll consider each of these relationships in turn.

Before God's Throne

When the prodigal son of Jesus's famous parable (Luke 15:11–32) requested his inheritance, he was essentially asking his father to declare himself dead. Leaving home, the son used the inheritance to enjoy all the pleasures money could buy—until he went broke. The son then descended into poverty and disgrace, eventually envying the food of pigs. The story to this point illustrates the plight of humanity, captured by our own sin and needing a Savior (Rom. 1:18–32).

Having severed his family ties and squandered his inheritance, the son finally considered returning home. But he knew that while the pigpen could be left behind, the stench of shame would follow him. Because there was no earthly reason to believe he would be restored to his father, he was prepared to relinquish his position as a son and be accepted as a mere servant.

Destitute and broken, the son began the long, homeward journey. The words that follow, however, are among the most beautiful in Scripture. Jesus says, "But while he was still a long way off, his father saw him and felt compassion, and ran and embraced him and kissed him" (Luke 15:20). With a decisive love that defies our expectations, the father rushed to his bedraggled son, embraced him, and clothed him with honor.

Demoralized by shame, we too approach the Father in poverty of spirit, confessing our sin and unworthiness. And, likewise, he embraces us not as servants but as beloved sons and daughters. This astounding reality gives us a durable hope. As the psalmist declares, "O Israel, hope in the LORD! For with the LORD there is steadfast love, and with him is plentiful redemption" (Ps. 130:7).[13] Hope, after all, is a form of poverty. Hoping means that instead of grasping and possessing, we wait for God's provision. In the words of Paul, "For in this hope we were saved. Now hope that is seen is not hope. For who hopes for what he sees? But if we hope for what we do not see, we wait for it with patience" (Rom. 8:24–25).

To be poor in spirit is to recognize, as in Luther's parable, that God's steadfast love is the only true basis of our hope.

Relating to One's Neighbor

This hope is needed in full strength today. Anyone half awake these days recognizes that we have a problem. As the world increasingly shifts under our feet, loud voices are shouting down the sinister Other—the malefactors who are deconstructing life as we know it. We use inflammatory speech against our foes, driven by a big dose of adrenaline. Categorical in our denunciations, we seem to find this spleen-venting exercise to be a necessary catharsis.

By contrast, we observe the way Jesus addressed the hostilities of his day. He consistently embodied humility and warmhearted affection toward others. Never did he incite the poor and oppressed to foment a rebellion. He did not assemble a cache of weapons or prepare a company of commandos for toppling the current order. In words that likely enraged the Zealots, he told his followers, "Love your enemies" (Matt. 5:44).

Jesus's response to hostility was often misunderstood by his contemporaries. Many of them expected a deliverer like Joshua or David, a military commander who would vanquish the Romans and establish an earthly kingdom. Instead, he became known as a friend of tax collectors—a circle of traitors who aligned with the political enemy. And of a certain Roman centurion he provocatively stated, "Truly, I tell you, with no one in Israel have I found such faith" (Matt. 8:10).

In keeping with our Savior's example, we don't always need to defend ourselves or have the final word. Christians who are poor in spirit can live with being maligned and misunderstood. We can be like Jesus before Herod Antipas—silent. Such poverty is essential when we are tempted to excoriate our "enemy" who thinks differently about a social or political issue. As Jesus told Pilate, "My kingdom is not of this world. If my kingdom were of this world, my servants would have been fighting. . . . But my kingdom is not from the world" (John 18:36).

Poverty in the Church

Yet, loving our neighbors is not the only task ahead of us. We must also do the same in our own churches, which can sometimes feel like an even harder feat. I'm not a bishop, but I spend a lot of time talking with pastors, and these conversations currently reveal dangerous levels of disillusionment. According to a Barna report published on November 16, 2021, 38 percent of U.S. pastors have thought about quitting full-time ministry in the past year.[14] This comes after many months of quarantining and isolation, which has produced a deluge of mental health issues (including anxiety, depression, and suicidal ideation), bitter division concerning virus mitigation policies, and financial strain. Add to the equation political dissention and culture wars and it is no surprise that we have an alarming percentage of weary pastors who are considering a departure from ministry.

In this context, the problem is compounded by the way churches sometimes strive toward prominence. Emotional or affective marketing campaigns often use technology in ways that engage people at visceral, rather than cognitive, levels. Video filters, lighting, fog machines, pacing, and musical chords are employed to stimulate a euphoric high that increasingly struggles to accommodate the impoverished spirit. Add to this a corporate model of ministry that defines success by numerical growth and nurtures larger-than-life celebrity pastors and it's no wonder that we have a problem with authoritarian and abusive leadership styles that cause churches to rise and fall.

Whether it's among pastors facing discouragement or in churches that are overly indebted to the marketing methods of the corporate world, Jesus's call to spiritual poverty provides a wisdom that takes us by the hand and guides us through the minefield of ambition and vanity. It does this by shaping our mission, objectives, and methods of ministry according to the humble character of the servant Savior who did not exploit his deity but instead humbled himself to the point of death.

Good News of the Kingdom

As mentioned earlier, Jesus emerged from the water of baptism to announce the "good news" of God's reign, also called the "kingdom of heaven" (Matt. 4:17). In that day, "kingdom" had social, political, and religious overtones, for it was a movement that transcended one's private spirituality. To proclaim the good news of another kingdom, then, was a socially subversive act that recognized a competing loyalty to the rule of Caesar.

For the poor in spirit, however, this subversion is not aimed at consolidating personal power and influence; it is about submitting oneself to the true King. Our covetous striving for more and more is to be reordered according to a new ethic. "For where your treasure is," said Jesus, "there your heart will be also" (Matt. 6:21). This new treasure is none other than the King himself—the God of heaven and earth—who loves us beyond description, however much we may feel shame and regret. Such love compels us to proclaim the good news of the kingdom.

Given its countercultural trajectory, God's kingdom required citizens to analyze the countervailing "gospel" proclaimed by society, a call to discipleship that recognizes and responds to the supremacy of Christ over every dimension of human experience. Ethnicity, cultural affiliation, and socio-economic status are no longer the most important ties that unite us. Now, as royal subjects, we are bound by a greater purpose—to "proclaim the excellencies of him who called [us] out of darkness into his marvelous light" (1 Pet. 2:9). It's no accident that the "kingdom of heaven" bookends the Beatitudes (Matt. 5:3, 10), thus stressing our calling to live in this world's empire as citizens who belong to another King.

This was Mike Vetrone's legacy, the mentor I mentioned earlier. And it was especially clear in the final Bible study he presented that summer, a message from Matthew 13:31–32. There Jesus says, "The kingdom of heaven is like a grain of mustard seed. . . . It is the smallest of all seeds, but when it has grown it is larger than all the garden plants and becomes a tree, so that the birds of the air come and make nests in its branches."

After reading the text, Mike displayed a picture of a mustard seed from his study Bible and asked us to imagine it having fallen to the ground somewhere, unnoticed by birds or human beings. Over time, he explained, the seed sprouted into a large bush, so lush and expansive that the birds of the air nested in its branches. "God's kingdom is like that," he suggested with a tear in his eye (Mike often got emotional when talking about Scripture). "It has such an obscure beginning that people disregard and disparage it. But against all odds, God's kingdom grows and spreads, comforting the weary, the poor, and the hopeless."

At this point he looked at me. I imagine it's because I was about to return to Bible college and prepare for ministry. He said,

> This is how Jesus was born, unnoticed by the world. And it's also the way he departed—progressively abandoned, first by Peter and then by Judas. Next came the Jewish leaders and people who cried "crucify him." Then there was Pontius Pilate, representing the pagan world. Finally, upon the cross, stripped of all dignity, Jesus cried out to the Father, "My God, my God, why have you forsaken me?"

This, friends, is the counterintuitive turn of the kingdom, the impoverished experience to which we're called—weak, rejected, and alone, and yet not abandoned, because the Lord has promised to sustain us. We appear, in the world's eyes, as a pathetic spectacle; but, all the while, God is at work in our poverty. "Blessed are the poor in spirit, for theirs is the kingdom of heaven" (Matt. 5:3).

2

When Loss Becomes Gain

Blessed are those who mourn, for they shall be comforted.

MATTHEW 5:4

CONSIDER GIOVANNA, a resident of Castelvetrano in 1902. She sits on her doorstep under the blazing sun, clothed in rags, her face yellowed by malaria. Her brown eyes are melancholy, and her swollen stomach is drawn tight like a drum. Inside the home is Giovanna's older sister, Teresa, who lies on the floor beneath a torn blanket, undernourished, teeth chattering from fever. An inescapable pessimism defines their reality, a product of starvation's stranglehold.

Made desperate by their unending destitution, enterprising peasants in Castelvetrano heard about *La Merica* and began to look for a long-term solution beyond the Sicilian shore. Men usually went first. Their wives hung on to the trains departing from the station—a gesture of their affection and a recognition that such goodbyes were likely final. Hunger, seasickness, and sorrow defined each transatlantic journey. Immigrants arriving in New York found dark, overcrowded tenements, rife with tuberculosis and typhoid. Food was scarce. Daily sustenance typically consisted of the *acqua sale*—stale bread moistened in boiling water with a bit of salt and olive oil for flavor.

New York, the cradle of opportunity, offered to liberate immigrants from the shackles of poverty, but not without its own path of misery—a great swirl of hope and adversity, gold and dirt, pathos and pity. For most people it was menial and demoralizing drudgery. Over time, this grind gives way to a mournful lament, half angry and half supplicating. This chapter considers how such mourning becomes the route to divine comfort.[1]

The Anatomy of Mourning

There is an undeniable earthiness to suffering, a physicality to pain that penetrates to our core. The Italian word *miseria* envisions such an experience—poverty, emptiness, barrenness, destitution; overall, a scarcity of resources that leads one to mourn. Philosopher and theologian Nicholas Wolterstorff, grieving the death of his son, describes its universal scope:

> Suffering keeps its face hid from each while making itself known to all. . . . We are one in suffering. Some are wealthy, some are bright; some athletic, some admired. But we all suffer. For we all prize and love; and in this present existence of ours, prizing and loving yield suffering.[2]

With suffering comes mourning. It is captured in Masaccio's haunting painting of the expulsion of Adam and Eve from the

Garden—Adam covering his face in shame; Eve, with her mouth agape in shock, shouting in horror and covering her breasts. Their misery is palpable. Having turned away from the light of God's presence, the first couple chooses instead to walk into the darkness of their own shadows. Now, with the light of God's presence behind them, they enter deeper dimensions of misery.

Every agonizing challenge, devastating disease, and tedious day finds its genesis in this moment of humanity's rebellion against God (Rom. 5:12). Every heartbreaking valley and dry desert road originated in Adam's act of treason—all fear, loneliness, anxiety, and even death itself. And to think, it all began with a mere flicker of discontent. That flicker is now a universal blaze, one that involves all three dimensions of suffering, physical, psychological, and social:

> **Physical**: With sweat on their brows, the first couple encountered fatigue, hunger, nakedness, exposure, sinus infections, cavities, and other maladies.
>
> **Psychological**: They would know the suffocation of loneliness, alienation, addiction, anxiety, shame, regret, depression, and despair. They knew sleepless nights and, with the psalmist, they would exclaim, "My companions have become darkness" (Ps. 88:18).
>
> **Social**: Sin corrupted, undermined, and even destroyed their relationships. All manner of social conflict suddenly entered the picture: resentment, envy, animosity, impatience, bullying, one-upmanship, abuse, and rage. Such is the legacy we have inherited and now perpetuate in our worldy societies, what Augustine called "the City of Man."[3]

These ingredients comprise the cocktail called misery. When Providence forces us to swallow it, we can do so either with bitterness, a detached stoicism, or acceptance of our pain and loss. When we choose to respond in faith, we begin the process of mourning. Only then can we appreciate Jesus's promise, "Blessed are those who mourn, for they shall be comforted" (Matt. 5:4).

No Time to Mourn

Over the centuries, Christians have encouraged one another to embrace misery as part of life. "*Memento mori*," they said—remember death. But this habit is becoming increasingly uncommon. "Few of us," notes J. I. Packer, "live daily on the edge of eternity in [a] conscious way . . . and we lose out as a result."[4]

As though fleeing an attacker, we try to escape the melancholy and heartache that follow hard on our heels. We surround ourselves with clichés such as "Don't worry, be happy" or "Life is good," but such well-intentioned psychology fails to deliver. We seclude ourselves from others; but isolation, it turns out, also separates us from faith, hope, and love, to say nothing of joy. Try as we may to deny our emotions and deaden our pain, our hearts remain vulnerable.

This aversion to mourning is also evident in church life. A positive and encouraging attitude is often promoted to the degree that sorrow is regarded as the enemy of joy. We have apparently forgotten the Pauline admonition to "weep with those who weep" (Rom. 12:15). Cornelius Plantinga Jr. therefore rightly wonders, "What would St. Paul make of worship without lament, of pelvic thrusting praise teams and beaming ministers on their barstools, swapping stories and jokes with an applauding audience and announcing 'top ten' listings borrowed from Letterman?"[5]

Perpetual positivity leaves one ill-equipped to embody the character of Christ's kingdom, to showcase the healing presence of the Spirit. For that matter, so does the opposite extreme, what Martyn Lloyd-Jones has labeled "false puritanism."[6] Such a person seeks to project piety by always looking miserable. Instead of denying his grief, this modern-day martyr wears it on his sleeve.

Yet, this attitude seems to be less prevalent than the general public's avoidance of pain and suffering. This is observed, for instance, in our relationship to sickness and death. People today live much longer and are spared many of the indignities of previous generations.[7] Consequently, we tend to hide suffering and death from public view. No longer, for instance, do we nurse grandparents through the process of dying (once again, consider the physical, psychological, and social implications). We outsource their care to the professionals, sheltering them in hospitals and nursing facilities. When they die, we see their body in a funeral parlor, which is decorated to resemble one's home with furniture, draperies, and knickknacks. We have thus succeeded in shielding our children from suffering, but we have unwittingly deprived them of *God's* comfort.

We must therefore relearn how to mourn.

The Shape of Lament

Life is fragile and brief. According to the psalmist, our lifetimes are a "mere breath" (Ps. 39:11). We may perhaps live into our seventies or eighties "by reason of strength," but our experience is generally full of "toil and trouble" (Ps. 90:10). Sometimes life leaves us weeping in the dark. You've never had a ring on your finger or a child in your womb or a title by your name and exclaimed, "Why, O Lord?"[8] But in our painful moments, we find comfort in the psalms of lament. Comprising forty percent of the Psalter, these precious words of mourning cry from the valley where pilgrims find their hearts aching. Consider the following passages:

> Out of the depths I cry to you, O LORD!
>> O Lord, hear my voice!
> Let your ears be attentive
>> to the voice of my pleas for mercy! (Ps. 130:1–2)

> I am weary with my moaning;
>> every night I flood my bed with tears;
>> I drench my couch with my weeping.
> My eye wastes away because of grief;
>> it grows weak because of all my foes. (Ps. 6:6–7)

> O Lord, all my longing is before you;
>> my sighing is not hidden from you.
> My heart throbs; my strength fails me,
>> and the light of my eyes—it also has gone from me.
> My friends and companions stand aloof from my plague,
>> and my nearest kin stand far off. (Ps. 38:9–11)

> Why are you cast down, O my soul,
>> and why are you in turmoil within me?
> Hope in God; for I shall again praise him,
>> my salvation and my God. (Ps. 42:11)

In moments of misery, we cry out to a Father who cares about our pain, who invites us into his presence to express our concerns

(Matt. 7:7–11; 1 Pet. 5:7). In view of this reality, theologian Kelly M. Kapic has offered a helpful framework for understanding and expressing biblical lament:

1. A cry out to God: "My God, My God, why have you forsaken me?"
2. A complaint or voicing of the crisis that drives the poem: "Why are you so far from saving me, from the words of my groaning? . . . All who see me mock me."
3. A petition in which remedy is yearned for: "Be not far from me, for trouble is near, and there is none to help."
4. Often (though not always!) a claim of confidence in God: "All the ends of the earth shall remember and turn to the Lord."
5. Often (though not always!) a commitment to praise God: "I will tell of your name to my brothers; in the midst of the congregation I will praise you."[9]

"These cries," writes Kapic, "do not form a subversive anti-religious voice but operate at the heart of the biblical canon among the prayers and songs of the people of God. They are part of their liturgy and worship."[10] To ignore the need for such lament is to live in denial, overlooking the simple facts that life is messy, we are weak, and God is merciful. It also fails to recognize lament's redemptive value.

The Redemptive Value of Mourning

A day comes after age thirty when we wake and realize we are being swept along in a one-way flow of time that eats away at our youthful agilities and opportunities. Worse still, we recognize the trajectory that brings us ever closer to death, the so-called "king of terrors" (Job 18:14). Death made even the courageous David exclaim, "Fear and trembling come upon me, and horror overwhelms me" (Ps. 55:5). Paul deemed it the "last enemy" (1 Cor. 15:26).

Sometimes our encounter with mortality comes more subtly. In *The Sacrament of Evangelism*, Jerry Root and Stan Guthrie write of the inexorable passage of time:

> Have you ever returned home for a class reunion? You go back to familiar places, only to discover that what you were longing for has changed. The old, vacant lots where you used to play baseball now have buildings. The familiar landmarks have been torn down to make way for new structures that don't seem to fit, at least not in your memory, and therefore either they or you are out of place. You visit the old elementary school playground. It seemed to stretch the width of a degree of longitude when you were young. Now it seems so cramped that you wonder how you ever managed. At the reunion, you discover that the others who have come look strangely weathered. Fortunately the name tags have old yearbook photos affixed. The men are variously bald, fat, wrinkled, or sporting fringes of gray. The women are mostly unrecognizable. Clearly, life has been hard on the lot of them. You, of course, are fine![11]

Such weathering, unless the Lord comes first, leads to only one destination—the grave. Early in my pastoral ministry, I imagined the closing moments of life for believers as offering rapturous visions of beatific blessedness, sort of like Stephen's experience in

Acts 7. But I soon learned how misguided I was. I was unprepared for the enemy's cruelties—the unnatural and grotesque, the raw indignities and painful miseries that attend one's exit from the City of Man. I began visiting a forty-year-old woman who was fighting cancer. As this vital saint's body wasted to a skeletal shadow, I learned how death consumes every shred of life, a destruction that no embalmer can restore.

This reality is especially vexing in our age of scientific breakthrough and advancement—we can explode through the earth's atmosphere and yet find ourselves summarily halted by the mystery of death. Brain scans have replaced mirrors held before one's mouth and mortuary cosmetics have superseded pennies on the eyelids but death's relentless intrusion continues unabated. Try as we might to avoid it, death awaits all of us, a fact corroborated by children each evening when they kneel beside their beds and pray, "If I should die before I wake, I pray the Lord, my soul to take."[12] In this way, every nap anticipates death, a foreshadowing of the real thing.[13]

So, yes, the reality of death is vexing; but it's also valuable. You may know that Jonathan Edwards made a regular practice of considering his mortality, expressing his resolution "to think much on all occasions of [his] own dying, and of the common circumstances which attend death."[14] From such reflection, Edwards found spiritual clarity and inspiration, a blessed liberation from the ephemeral distractions that keep us from intimacy with Christ.

In this vein, I remember childhood friends sharing the popular Yiddish blessing, "May you live till a hundred and twenty." It's a lovely expression that envisions a strong and fruitful life, inspired by Deuteronomy 34:7, "Moses was 120 years old when he died. His eye was undimmed, and his vigor unabated."[15] Some, however, have turned the blessing around, suggesting that in the waning of our strength and dimming of our eyesight, we grow in our capacity to encounter God's empowering presence. In other words, in our mourning we receive the gift of divine comfort.

The Promise of God's Comfort

Of all the artistic expressions of divine comfort in Western history, George Frederic Handel's *Messiah* offers one of the most poignant.[16] It is among the longest-running pieces of music in history, performed in concert halls, churches, and even malls where "spontaneous" hallelujah choruses erupt and then go viral on YouTube. It begins with gloom and despair, an expression of Israel's condition in Isaiah 1–39. Dan Block writes, "In these chapters the prophet Isaiah declares over and over again that because of the hardness of Israel's heart . . . Yahweh was about to bring in his foreign agents of judgment."[17] This is the "distress and darkness, the gloom of anguish" of exile, the "thick darkness" into which the nation was thrust on account of her sins (Isa. 8:22).

Hebrew Scripture conveys this place of suffering with a host of evocative metaphors. The psalmist, for example, describes it as the "pit of destruction" and the "miry bog" (Ps. 40:2), a place of fear and confusion. One thinks of the images found in Job, everything from ashes, to pounded clay, to ground dust, to quivering prey before a predatory animal. These and other metaphors describe all manner of physical, psychological, and relational suffering. In the words of John Bunyan, it is the deadly, dark dungeon of Doubting Castle into which Giant Despair threw Christian, a gloomy place that is sometimes described by the Hebrew word "sheol."[18] Consider, for instance, Psalm 107:19–20:

Then they cried to the LORD in their trouble,
 and he delivered them from their distress.
He sent out his word and healed them,
 And delivered them from their destruction [sheol].

The anguished realm of sheol is not quite "hell" in the way we often imagine. It is, rather, a taste of death amid the painful realities of life. Or maybe death's shadow is a better description. Thus, the poor and needy, says the psalmist, cry out to the Lord and are delivered "from the depth of Sheol" (Ps. 86:1, 13). So did Jonah cry from within the claustrophobic horror of the fish:

I called out to the LORD, out of my distress,
 and he answered me;
out of the belly of sheol I cried,
 and you heard my voice. (Jonah 2:2)

In this sense, sheol may be understood as an inability to look beyond the terrorizing threat that stands before us. It is fear, intimidation, angst. A more subtle version of the experience, but no less significant, is expressed by the Greek word *merimnaō*. Translated as "anxious," it is the worrisome feeling in the pit of your stomach that keeps you up at night. Based on the word's usage, it appears to gather meaning from *merizō* "to divide" and *nous* "mind." This divided mind is the unhappy condition of the man whom the apostle James describes as "double-minded, unstable in all his ways" (James 1:8)—he obsessively focuses on some fearful prospect to the exclusion of God. In such moments, the sick feeling and shortness of breath confirm that flaming darts have pierced our spiritual armor. Such anxiety is a leading cause of our mourning.

This brings us back to Handel's *Messiah*. Against the morose and melancholy mood of the opening symphonic overture comes the radiant promise of Isaiah 40:1–2:

> Comfort, comfort my people, says your God.
> Speak tenderly to Jerusalem,
>   and cry to her
> that her warfare is ended,
>   that her iniquity is pardoned,
> that she has received from the LORD's hand
>   double for all her sins.

This hope, of course, was precisely the way the Messiah would come—the consoler, the comforter of Israel. Isaiah 49:13 says:

> Sing for joy, O heavens, and exult, O earth;
>   break forth, O mountains, into singing!
> For the Lord has comforted his people
>   and will have compassion on his afflicted.

So, what is this comfort and how do we experience it, especially in the crucible?

The Suffering God Who Comforts

Last year, as my son and I went to see Camerata Chicago's performance of *Messiah*, I was (as usual) simultaneously ruminating on my sermon, a message from Luke 2:25–35 where old

Simeon encounters baby Jesus in the temple. I imagined Mary carrying her newborn babe and Joseph holding turtle doves as they entered the sacred precincts. I was struck by the irony: while they couldn't afford to purchase a sacrificial lamb, they held the Lamb of God.

Then I imagined old Simeon, stooped and graying, scanning the crowd through his dim eyes. We know little about the man except that he was righteous, devout, and awaiting the "consolation" of Israel (Luke 2:25). And that is the point. The long-anticipated consolation of Simeon was nothing less than the "consolation" or "comfort" of which Isaiah spoke. As Handel's oratorio proclaims, "Say unto the cities of Judah, Behold your God!"[19]

Just a few minutes into the concert, it dawned on me. The blessed old man who clung to God's redemptive promise found its ultimate fulfillment as he looked at the baby. Staring into the newborn's face, he beheld the eyes of the all-seeing God. From whatever infant sounds may have emerged from the child's mouth, Simeon heard the primal voice that spoke creation into existence. On the tiny hand that may have rested upon Simeon's beard was the finger of God that carved the words of the covenant into stone at Sinai. Finally! Salvation had come.

But, as we've considered, its coming was thoroughly counter-intuitive. The kingdom would come not in a freedom fighter, king, or political movement, but in a vulnerable infant. The irony, however, is even deeper than that. After blessing baby Jesus, old Simeon told Mary, "Behold, this child is appointed for the fall and rising of many in Israel, and for a sign that is opposed (and a sword will pierce through your own soul also), so that thoughts from many hearts may be revealed" (Luke

2:34–35). In other words, this promised Son would one day endure an unjust trial before a bloodthirsty crowd. Men and women—created by his hand—would laugh at his pain. Those he came to save would scorn and crucify him. And sweet Mary would observe it all, mourning.

This suffering was the hallmark of Jesus's life. "He was despised and rejected by men," says Isaiah, "a man of sorrows and acquainted with grief" (Isa. 53:3). We are told that "he learned obedience through what he suffered" (Heb. 5:8). The shortest verse of the Bible captures this counterintuitive reality in just two words, "Jesus wept" (John 11:35). This brief statement has instigated some of the deepest theological reflection. Linguists and literary scholars have analyzed these words to understand how such basic syntax can make such a profound point. Poets and painters and songwriters have sought to plumb its depths, but they can't—because God has wept.

But Jesus didn't simply weep; he embraced our misery—physically, at the hands of guards who pressed thorns upon his brow, who blindfolded, struck, and mocked him; psychologically, hanging from the cross, just a few inches from the ground; and socially, as bystanders jeered and derided him, saying, "He saved others . . . but he can't save himself" (Matt. 27:42 NIV). Our God knows firsthand the overwhelming nature of pain and suffering, not hypothetically, but personally and directly. Jesus's tears were real.

But this wasn't the worst of it.

Above the powers of darkness—wicked Pilate, hateful Caiaphas, envious priests, and barbarous soldiers—was the most formidable threat of all: the God who determined from before time that this

Lamb would be slain (Rev. 13:8). As Isaiah 53:10 foresaw, "It was the will of the LORD to crush him; [to] put him to grief."

This is the apex of misery, or should we say, the lowest ebb. From the cross, Jesus looked heavenward and saw nothing but darkness. The one who had enjoyed perfect intimacy with the Father was suddenly, completely alone.

There is no getting around it. As long as we traverse the gritty, nail-strewn pathways of this broken world, we will suffer and mourn. But instead of fleeing in despair, let us approach the one who weeps with us, who identified with us to the point of a wretched death, who intercedes for us through our darkest nights of the soul.

To approach the victorious Savior in this way, says Mark Talbot, demonstrates that one is "awaiting the dawn."[20] The fact is,

> We will almost surely grieve the loss of some of those whom we love. Sinful temptations that we must resist will plague us, perhaps for our whole lives. Sometimes we will suffer from loneliness or difficult relationships. We may spend our lifetimes in wearisome, unfulfilling jobs. Some of us will be beset with physical, mental, and psychological maladies that undermine our ability to live ordinary lives.[21]

However, we don't suffer alone. Christ abides with us. Other helpers fail and comforts flee, but the Lord remains. His divine presence, which now resides in our hearts, will soon fill the universe, a radiance that will vanquish every diabolical shadow forever. On that day, "the sun of righteousness will arise with healing in its wings" (see Mal. 4:2), and all will be made new. "He will wipe away every tear from their eyes, and death shall be no more, neither shall there be mourning, nor crying, nor pain anymore, for the former things [will] have passed away" (Rev. 21:4).

Yes, "blessed are those who mourn, for they shall be comforted" (Matt. 5:4).

3

Gentleness in a Hostile World

Blessed are the meek, for they shall inherit the earth.

MATTHEW 5:5

A TERRIFYING BURST of arrows was the preamble to Constantine's slow and steady advancement. With swords and javelins drawn, the army made its way toward Rome. Constantine was marching to the battle of Milvian Bridge (October 28, 312), an event that changed your life, whether you know it or not.

After consolidating power in Britain, Gaul, and the Germanic provinces, the would-be usurper cast his eye upon the throne of the Western Roman Empire. All that stood in the way was the current emperor, Maxentius, who was supported by forces of Italy, Corsica, Sardinia, Sicily, and North Africa.

In the city of Verona, Maxentius's stronghold in northern Italy, Constantine led a personal attack that demonstrated his military genius and heroic character. Victorious, he then traveled southward for the decisive battle. Meanwhile, Maxentius hunkered down within the gates of the Eternal City among his protective troops, a refuge in which he probably should have remained, except that he had read a pagan oracle that prophesied the "enemy of the Romans" would perish.[1] Applying the prophecy to the threat now before him, Maxentius advanced his troops to the Tiber River outside of Rome.

According to the church historian Eusebius (d. 339), a day before the battle, about the time of the midday sun, Constantine claimed to have seen a vision instructing him to fight in the name of the Christian God. Seeing an illumined cross in the sky, he heard the words "In this [sign], conquer."[2] That night, he dreamed that Christ instructed him to use the sign of the cross against his enemies, which Constantine did by having his soldiers mark their shields with this Christian symbol.

On the fateful day, Constantine's army arrived at the battlefield. His troops quickly routed their opponents, driving them to the Tiber River. Recognizing his defeat, Maxentius fled. But when his retreating army-turned-mob pressed through the narrow passage across the water, he was forced into the river, where he drowned under the weight of his armor.

Constantine attributed his victory to the God of the Christians. The next year he issued the Edict of Milan (313), granting freedom of worship and ending the persecution of the church throughout his empire. A new era was underway.

A Muscular Christianity

From that day on, the name Constantine would be associated with religious freedom. But ironically, Constantine also represents a muscular Christianity that rules by coercion, intimidation, and even violence, wielding the sword in the name of Christ. It was a pattern that, tragically, would be repeated down through church history.

While the world has witnessed inspiring movements of mercy in church history, too often the body of Christ has displayed the resentment of Cain, defacing and destroying brothers and neighbors for all kinds of reasons. The wheat and the tares have grown up together, creating a decidedly mixed legacy.

There are many ugly examples. Most students of history will probably think of the Crusades. In 1095, Pope Urban II called for a Crusade to reclaim Jerusalem by slaughtering Muslims who occupied the area, a call that elicited an emphatic response from the assembled crowd who shouted, "God wills it!"[3]

With the same crusading spirit, many conquistadores sought to spread Christianity through the Americas at the point of a sword—a horrific story of brutality in the name of Jesus in which Spanish and Portuguese soldiers tortured natives in pursuit of gold.

The Thirty Years' War (1618–1648) also comes to mind, a gruesome episode when Catholics and Protestants met each other on the field of battle (often wielding crude weapons), resulting in upwards of eight million casualties.

Given this record of infamy, then, we are bound to ask the question: What is the proper role of authority in the Christian life, the marshaling of "power from on high" (Luke 24:49) by which the kingdom advances in this world?

In a word, it is meekness.

Meekness Defined

What is meekness? It is gentleness. Modesty. Self-effacement. According to John Calvin, the meek are "the calm and quiet ones, who are not easily provoked by wrongs, who do not sulk over offences, but are more ready to endure everything, than pay the wicked the same back."[4] This disposition, says Thomas Watson, is showcased in our calling to emulate the patient and sensitive example of Jesus expressed in 1 Peter 2:23: "When he was reviled, he reviled not again."[5] Similarly, Peter Kreeft suggests that "to see what meekness is, you must look not at meekness but at Christ. Saying meekness is this or that sends you to concepts which are copies of reality. Saying, 'Jesus is meek' sends you to the living reality himself."[6]

Observe Jesus speaking with such tenderness to the Samaritan woman (John 4:1–42). He first notices her sorrow and thirstiness of soul and then addresses her need with the promise of "living water" (John 4:10). Watch Jesus climbing a mountain by himself, to be alone with his Father in prayer (Matt. 14:23). Look at him approaching the Holy City with a tear in his eye, saying, "O Jerusalem, Jerusalem. . . . How often would I have gathered your children together as a hen gathers her brood under her wings, and you were not willing!" (Matt. 23:37). Or see him with Thomas after the resurrection (John 20:24–29). Jesus doesn't chastise Thomas; instead, he invites this wavering disciple to encounter the gospel and believe.

That's the heartbeat of meekness—the self-giving love of God; Christ willingly laying down his life. But meekness must not be confused with weakness. With fire in his eyes, Jesus also overturned money-changing tables (John 2:13–16) and confronted the hypocritical Pharisees. With inexpressible courage he endured the cross. Given this example, I offer the following definition of meekness: gentle strength, governed by the Holy Spirit.

A Sure Inheritance

In a confused world that celebrates masculine icons such as John Wayne, Clint Eastwood, and Dwayne Johnson and then promptly cancels them as toxic, we need a different model. We need to resist the polarities of passivity and sloth on one hand and pugnacity and bullying on the other. We need Christ's combination of strength and gentleness, a delicate balance that comes by recognizing we are citizens of another kingdom, a different world whose designer and builder is God (Heb. 11:10).

Jesus promises such a world to his followers. The verb translated as "inherit" points to a firm possession, a gift that God places into our hands. But what exactly does it mean to possess the earth? This is where Psalm 37 is helpful. In similar language, it speaks of the meek inheriting the land (of Israel). Why does God provide this inheritance? See if you can find the answer. As you read it, try to identify the quality of the meek that obtains God's blessing.

Psalm 37:1–11

Fret not yourself because of evildoers;
   be not envious of wrongdoers!
For they will soon fade like the grass
   and wither like the green herb.

Trust in the LORD, and do good;
   dwell in the land and befriend faithfulness.
Delight yourself in the LORD,
   and he will give you the desires of your heart.

Commit your way to the LORD;
   trust in him, and he will act.
He will bring forth your righteousness as the light,
   and your justice as the noonday.

Be still before the LORD and wait patiently for him;
   fret not yourself over the one who prospers in his way,
   over the man who carries out evil devices!

Refrain from anger, and forsake wrath!
   Fret not yourself; it tends only to evil.
For the evildoers shall be cut off,
   but those who wait for the LORD shall inherit the land.

In just a little while, the wicked will be no more;
   though you look carefully at his place, he will not be
      there.
But the meek shall inherit the land
   and delight themselves in abundant peace.

What makes these people meek? This psalm tells us that the blessed meek are those who trust in the Lord. They turn from anger. They don't fret but rather wait patiently—and God rewards them with the promised land.

Do you remember how this dynamic is expressed in the old covenant? In Deuteronomy 28–32, for example, God outlines the terms of his relationship with Israel, promising blessings if his people walk with him. If they obey the Lord and follow his commands, they will be blessed—blessed with peace, abundance, victory over their enemies, prosperity, fertility, and God's abiding presence. In short, Israel will enjoy divine favor.

But if the people reject his word and worship the gods of the nations, they will be cursed with confusion, drought, infertility, locust, plague, destruction, desolation, and eventual exile (Deut. 28:15–19).

Notice, however, that our beatitude doesn't say "land." Jesus says the meek will inherit the "earth" (Matt. 5:5). Why? Because now, in the new covenant, God's blessing has been universalized. No longer is it limited to a particular ethnic group or region. Now the kingdom belongs to people from every tribe, tongue, and nation. Revelation 7:9 gives us a small picture of this glorious reality: "After this I looked, and behold, a great multitude that no one could number, from every nation, from all tribes and peoples and languages, standing before the throne and before the Lamb, clothed in white robes, with palm branches in their hands."

Because of Christ's sacrificial death and resurrection for sinners like you and me, Israel's sacrificial system—which all along pointed to what he would do on Calvary's hill—is over. The temple is no longer confined to a building. Now men and women in Christ are the temple, as Paul writes, "Do you not know that you are God's temple and that God's Spirit dwells in you?" (1 Cor. 3:16).

Given all this, when do men and women in Christ inherit the earth? Now or in the future? The answer, in keeping with the already-but-not-yet reality of the kingdom of God,[7] is *yes*. Our inheritance is now and then—in "this age and the age to come," as George Eldon Ladd memorably put it.[8] Looking specifically at the Beatitudes, Martyn Lloyd-Jones explains, "The meek already inherit the earth in this life for, as Paul says, 'All things are yours' (1 Cor. 3:21). But obviously it has a future reference also."[9] Lloyd-Jones then quotes Jesus's words about the future in Luke 14:11: "For everyone who exalts himself will be humbled, and he who humbles himself will be exalted."[10] This is the "glorious inheritance" we possess in Christ (Eph. 1:18)!

So, yes, the full inheritance is yet before us. But also, yes, the possession has begun in a catena of divine blessings such as a renewed heart (Rom. 5:5), an invitation to intimate communion with God (Ps. 63:1–11), a clear conscience (1 Tim. 1:5), peace (John 14:27), and spiritual fruit (Gal. 5:22–23). These are the blessings of the meek today, and they hint at the glorious future Christ's followers can expect when all is made new. The meek will inherit the earth.

A Countercultural Vision

But let's be clear. The notion that the meek will inherit the earth is altogether countercultural. The Psalm 37 vision of meekness is offensive, loathsome, and pathetic to many. Perhaps the greatest exponent of this conviction was Friedrich Nietzsche, who wrote, "I condemn Christianity; I bring against the Christian church the most terrible of all the accusations that an accuser has ever had in his mouth. It is, to me, the greatest of all imaginable corruptions."[11]

According to Nietzsche, Christianity is guilty of undermining the proper order of life by emasculating men, suppressing their "will to power."[12] Nietzsche's ideal human is not the meek servant but the warrior who dominates others. In his words, "Freedom means that the manly instincts which delight in war and victory dominate over other instincts. . . . the free man is a warrior."[13]

We can, at least, appreciate that Nietzsche didn't mince words. We can even sympathize with his concern over male weakness. Society today has bred legions of passive males who shirk responsibility, flee commitment, and only exercise courage and sacrifice in video games. Psychiatrist and author Richard W. Moscotti has seen many such men and likes to tell this story:

> For men, entry into heaven is through two gates—one marked for "passive, dependent males only," the other for "assertive, aggressive males only." On this particular day St. Peter surveyed the scene and found that the line outside the "passive" gate extended into infinity. But in front of the "assertive" gate was not a line, but a solitary man. "Why are you standing here all by yourself?" St. Peter asked. Answered the man: "Because my wife told me to."[14]

As Moscotti said, "a truly assertive man is hard to find."[15] Tragically, much the same could be said in many of our churches. While I have had the great privilege of knowing and working with more than a few strong, godly male leaders, I must admit that they have been the exception rather than the rule.[16] Across Christ's kingdom, we do not have nearly enough men willing to truly lead Christ's church. Instead, a large percentage of men sit back and wait for others to lead, to decide, and to carry on the work of the ministry. The church languishes—and the devil cackles.

Such men forget that Christ is a lion, a scourge on impotent religion, who calls his followers to engage in spiritual battle. Think of the spiritual armor of Ephesians (6:10–17), which includes the belt of truth, the breastplate of righteousness, gospel readiness as shoes, the shield of faith, the helmet of salvation, and the sword of the Spirit. Note that this list makes no provision for the rear, only the front, so a retreat into passivity is not an option. Christians, both men and women, are called to press forward.

Glenn T. Stanton, director of Global Family Formation Studies at Focus on the Family, has addressed the problem of male passivity. The problem, Stanton suggests, is that we're raising "passive males": men who are "not even sure what the right thing to do is, much less possess the courage and assertiveness to know when to demonstrate it or how."[17] Similarly, Canadian clinical psychologist and agent provocateur Jordan Peterson has said, "If you think tough men are dangerous, wait until you see what weak men are capable of."[18]

Weakness was a central part of Nietzsche's concern, a problem that, in his view, came from Christianity's emphasis on meekness, what he called a "sheeple" ethic, a doctrine that protects the weak to the demise of the strong.[19] Against this pathetic mode of life, says Nietzsche, an assertive will to dominate is vital for humanity's advancement.

But the weakness that Nietzsche critiques is nothing like Christian meekness. His bruising evaluation is no more than a pathetic parody of the gentleness prescribed by the New Testament.

So we find ourselves left with the two dominant positions on power: Nietzsche's warrior and Jesus Christ, the suffering servant who went to the cross. In Jesus, we have the meek, through whom God's gentle love extends. In Nietzsche's Übermensch (superman), we have the warrior who exercises a will to power.

Which power prevails when we feel anger rising in our hearts? When we're stung by envy or jealousy, or seized by some passion? When we're assaulted by temptation and feel the flames of lust beginning to burn? When we're confronted by the menagerie of selfishness and vice within, what prevails? As Pinckaers puts it:

> [We look within and] find the proud, domineering lion, the bragging rooster and the vain peacock, the flattering cat and the sly fox, the envious serpent and the possessive bear, the conceited magpie and the mocking monkey. We discover the brutal rhinoceros and the sluggish elephant, the scared rabbit and the sensual pig, the fierce dog and the gnawing worm, the stubborn mule and the porcupine. These are the shapes assumed by our self-love. . . . What power and firmness is needed, what clear-sightedness and skill, if we are going to control all these instincts, bring them to heel, and compel them to obey reason and charity! Complete self-mastery is a long and exacting work, only achieved by—meekness.[20]

Why do we admire the lion tamers so much? Their power lies not in violence—in raising their voice or making dramatic displays—but in a confident calmness, a meekness that somehow controls the ferocious animal. In words attributed to Dostoyevsky, "Loving humility is marvelously strong, the strongest of all things, and there is nothing else like it."[21]

The Big Obstacle to Meekness

As a pastor, I occupy a front-row seat to many occasions that cry out for meekness, for example:

- in a local church during a pandemic, when half of the congregation believes that true love requires Christians to stay home and flatten the curve while the other half insists faith requires worshiping without masks;
- in one's family, when it's time for an aged parent with Alzheimer's to enter an assisted living community;
- in the workplace, under an overbearing boss who only criticizes;
- or among neighbors with different visions of human flourishing—the one whose lawn sign says, "Make America Great Again," while the other flies a flag of rainbow colors.

Each of these scenarios offers an opportunity to embody meekness. But each scenario also poses a threat to meekness. Competing interests, personal pride, selfishness, limited knowledge, and simple blind spots are just a few of the reasons.[22] But if we were to dig below the surface to identify a basic, fundamental obstacle to meekness, we would likely uncover the problem of resentment.

Cornelius Plantinga Jr. defines resentment as a "special, and usually protracted, form of anger . . . aimed at what the angry person regards as unjust, insulting, or demeaning."[23] To be sure, on some occasions, such resentments are entirely justified. He illustrates:

In Montgomery, Alabama, in the forties, city fathers wrote municipal bus regulations to minimize proximity of black and white passengers. One of the regulations prohibited blacks from walking through the bus to their own seats since, to do so, they would have to pass through the white section and might accidentally make body contact with white passengers. Thus, in a demeaning alternative, blacks would pay their fare at the front, exit the bus, walk its length outdoors, and then reenter the vehicle at the rear. Inevitably, certain white bus drivers amused themselves by driving away before their black passengers could reboard. Of course, the trouble here was not that blacks got angry at such humiliation but rather that whites did not.[24]

But sometimes resentment metastasizes into a form of bitterness that doesn't allow for the possibility of repentance and reconciliation. It was Nietzsche who developed this notion in his political psychology. Using the French word "ressentiment," which includes the idea of anger mentioned above but also envy, hate, rage, and revenge, he explained how someone who lives with bitter animosity that cannot be expressed publicly for fear of recrimination becomes accustomed to manipulating opponents with a passive-aggressive application of guilt. James Davison Hunter helpfully explains:

> *Ressentiment* is grounded in a narrative of injury, or, at least, perceived injury; a strong belief that one has been or is being wronged. The root of this is a sense of entitlement. . . . The entitlement may be to greater respect, greater influence, or perhaps a better lot in life and it may draw from the past or the present. . . . In the end, these benefits have been withheld or taken away or there is a perceived threat that they will be taken away by those now in positions of power.[25]

A classic example of this phenomenon is found in Korah's rebellion, the event in Numbers 16 where certain leaders of Israel revolted against Moses. When Moses requested a meeting with two of these leaders, Dathan and Abiram, they responded with one of the worst passive aggressive responses ever: "We will not come up. Is it a small thing that you have brought us up out of a land flowing with milk and honey, to kill us in the wilderness, that you must also make yourself a prince over us?" (Num. 16:12–13). Yikes.

Do you see how this is ressentiment? Because Dathan and Abiram felt entitled to greater authority—something on par with Moses—they created a narrative of injury. With a high degree of temerity, they took God's promise about salvation from the anguished bondage of Egypt unto "a good and broad land, a land flowing with milk and honey" (Ex. 3:8; 17) and turned it around. In their mouth, Egypt was the lovely land full of milk and honey and their trek through the wilderness was an attempt on Moses's part (and on God's) to kill them. Is it any wonder the Lord's anger was kindled against them (Num. 16:31–35; 32:13)?

The practical significance of this idea cannot be overstated. We observe it in marriages in which one member feels like a victim—perhaps for good reason—but rather than dealing with the problem, decides to withhold communication (the silent treatment) or affection (for example, sex) to punish the other person. This dynamic also happens in churches, such as when a member is not hired for an office staff position she felt entitled to and then her spouse informs the pastor that the family is leaving because the pastor "doesn't really preach the gospel." It can get ugly.

An Inspiring Legacy to Emulate

How do we hold onto meekness—not as an unattainable ideal but as a practical, everyday reality? How do we manage to extinguish our smoldering resentment? It comes by understanding our identity in Christ—the embodiment of meekness—and our calling to manifest his meekness in the world.

We began this chapter looking at the culturally muscular Christianity of Constantine. Let us conclude with another historical figure, one who chose a countercultural path: Jackie Robinson.

Branch Rickey, president and general manager of the Brooklyn Dodgers, wanted to break the color barrier in professional baseball. He chose Robinson, an outstanding player in the Negro Leagues who had excelled in four sports while at UCLA. In their initial meeting, Rickey warned Robinson that he would face opposition from teammates, vituperative fans, and even opposing pitchers who might knock him down with a fastball.

In that meeting, Rickey asked Robinson if he would be able to endure all the harassment without losing his cool. It was a serious question. Robinson was competitive, strong, and aggressive. It wasn't natural for him to back down from anything. Foreshadowing the courage of Rosa Parks, he had nearly been court-martialed for refusing to move to the back of the bus during his military service. Yet Robinson responded to Rickey in the affirmative, a heroic resolution that broke baseball's ugly color barrier.

One of Robinson's teammates, pitcher Lee Pfund, was among the few players who befriended him. In an interview I conducted with Pfund a few years ago, he suggested that Robinson's earnest faith is a crucial part of his story. "What I found most inspiring," Pfund said, "was the way Jackie looked specifically to Christ as his example. . . . Never in all my years with him on and off the field did I see him lose his cool."[26] This gentle strength was on display for all to see, a meekness that ultimately was victorious.

How did Robinson do it? According to Pfund, this is the part of Jackie's story that's often overlooked. "Jackie Robinson was a sincere Christian," Pfund said, "who sought to emulate the example of Jesus."[27] In the face of injustice, he routinely quelled his righteous anger by remembering the one who said, "I am gentle and humble in heart" (Matt. 11:29 NIV); the one who was reviled "[but] did not revile in return; when he suffered . . . did not threaten; but . . . entrust[ed] himself to the one who judges justly" (1 Pet. 2:23).

In this historical moment, amid so much contention and strife, with battles raging on virtually every front, let's find inspiration in the example of Jackie Robinson, and ultimately in the one who said, "Blessed are the meek, for they shall inherit the earth" (Matt. 5:5).

4

Taste and See

Blessed are those who hunger and thirst for
righteousness, for they shall be satisfied.

MATTHEW 5:6

NINETEENTH-CENTURY New York offered to liberate Italian
immigrants from the shackles of injustice and poverty in their na-
tive land, but not without exacting a steep price. Hunger, illness,
and separation from loved ones created a survival-of-the-fittest
existence. As a young man, however, my grandfather Francesco
discovered the essential ingredients required for rising above these
circumstances: hard work and a fabulous tomato sauce recipe.
With this combination, he and his brother Vito started a restau-
rant and soon attracted customers.

My grandfather had a hunger and thirst for liberation that were
motivated by a desire deeper than survival. It reached back to the
family's nascent years in Castelvetrano, a town in southern Sicily

known for its olives, degradation, and extreme poverty. Nearly two decades had passed since his parents had immigrated, but the shards of humiliation remained embedded in their psyche, a mode of thinking and self-understanding reinforced in countless ways.

Success in *La Merica* was thus a way of closing a door on the dehumanizing past, a way to demonstrate one's worth. It wasn't so much an opportunity for material gain that fueled my grandfather's enterprising spirit. It was his hunger and thirst to climb out from the pit of humiliation and mark his achievement in the sight of family, friends, the world, and the angels.[1]

I am, of course, employing "hunger" in a figurative sense. All of us know what actual hunger feels like. As famished babies, we cried, and as ravenous adults, we may get irritable or, as they say, hangry. We also know the kind of hunger that compels us to make sacrifices and to achieve, a hunger that occupies our thoughts, shapes our vision, and gives rise to our ambitions.

Over time, this hunger shapes our identity. As physicians often say, "We are what we eat," an axiom that is equally true in the spiritual realm. So when we hunger for selfish gain, maintaining a diet of duplicity, materialism, and infidelity, we inevitably personify these qualities.[2] Like the food addict who consumes the entire canister of Pringles and then moves on to the tub of Breyers ice cream, we can slide from moral compromise into deeper patterns of self-destruction, including greed, lust, envy, and the other so-called deadly sins.[3]

How can we elevate our hunger for kingdom priorities, a longing for the good, the true, and the beautiful? In other words, a longing for God? How do we avoid the mental and emotional gluttony of this world—the malnourishment of soul that craves the next high, a spirituality du jour, a moral framework and lifestyle that makes sin appear normal and righteousness look strange?[4] Such questions need careful attention.

Philosopher James K. A. Smith addresses this problem of misguided appetites by emphasizing the necessity of "rehabituating" our hungers in order to submit our deepest longings and cravings to the lordship of Christ.[5] He writes:

> Indeed, in the Sermon on the Mount Jesus extols such hunger as "blessed." "Blessed are those who hunger and thirst for righteousness, for they will be filled" (Matt 5:6). And Jesus offers himself as the only satisfaction of such hunger: "I am the bread of life. Whoever comes to me will never go hungry, and whoever believes in me will never be thirsty" (John 6:35). If the heart is like a stomach . . . we could render Augustine's prayer in line with the metaphor: "You have made us for yourself, and our gut will rumble until we feed on you."[6]

This concept will sound familiar to anyone who has sincerely followed Jesus for longer than a month. But what does it mean to hunger and thirst for *righteousness*? We must begin by understanding this splendid word "righteousness" (also translated as "justice" in Hebrew and Greek).[7] Simply put, it is redeeming grace, a grace that blesses humanity where we need it most: in relation to God, in the renewal of our souls, and in the structures of society.[8] In other words, it has ramifications that are legal (before God's throne), moral (shaping our character), and social (in relation to the world).[9] What's amazing, though, is not simply that God imparts this gift, but also the way he does it—in a movement that transforms human appetites from the inside out.

The Righteousness of God

In her first novel, *Wise Blood*, Flannery O'Connor says of her character Hazel Motes that "there was a deep, black, wordless conviction in him that the way to avoid Jesus was to avoid sin."[10] Maybe you've thought this way before. It's among the most theologically naïve notions of human history. Here's the idea: as long as you manage to avoid conspicuous forms of sin, upholding a modicum of justice and perhaps even enriching the lives of others, you don't need to bother yourself with Jesus the Savior. Such people regard themselves as deserving of God's approval and the blessings that come with it.

But, of course, such people are pure fiction. Humanity is sinful by nature, a "mass of perdition," as Augustine put it.[11] Even the most kind and benevolent soul is incapable of living in continual conformity to the truth, beauty, and justice of God. Paul argues in Romans 1:18–3:20 that "all have sinned and fall short of the glory of God" (Rom. 3:23). "We sin," says Tony Lane, "not just from time to time, but consistently throughout our lives. We cannot escape from it and the whole of human nature is affected . . . our reason (Eph. 4:17), our will (John 8:34), our emotions and our feelings."[12]

Apart from Christ, we are guilty before God, broken, and corrupted. Try as we might, "all our righteous deeds," says the prophet, "are like a polluted garment" (Isa. 64:6). Even our best attempts will contaminate holiness in the same way adultery pollutes and splits a marriage. It ruptures loving bonds and brings alienation. "Failing to trust in the infinite God," says Plantinga, "we live anxiously, restlessly, always trying to secure and extend ourselves with finite goods that can't take the weight we put on them."[13] In short, we become increasingly lost.

A Longing for Righteousness

The life we desire slips through our fingers, just as it did for the men and women of Jesus's day. Most of them were common folk whose basic concern was survival. While different from us in countless ways, their lives were remarkably similar.

Political and social differences then, as now, were sharply divisive. No, they didn't have elections and officeholders like we do—but the personalities and policies of governance were every bit as contentious. Those who were pro-Roman firmly opposed Jewish nationalists. Others maintained loyalties to a particular ruling family, such as the Herodians. The line of division between Pharisees and Sadducees is infamous, as were distinctions between militant groups (the Zealots) and ascetic communities (such as the Essenes) of the Dead Sea area.

Take the Pharisees, for instance, and their attempt to maintain God's favor by meticulously exhibiting religious purity. They expounded God's law into 613 stipulations—248 commands and 365 prohibitions—and then surrounded these rules with over a thousand additional commands. To avoid violating the third commandment, "You shall not misuse the name of the LORD" (Ex. 20:7 NLT), they went so far as to refuse to utter God's name. To avoid the possibility of sexual temptation, they routinely lowered their heads when a woman passed by. According to

Jewish tradition, the most fastidious of them were called "bleeding Pharisees" because they often collided with walls.[14]

Faithful Jews of the first century, however, shared something in common. They longed for a new exodus, a day when thirsty souls would be satisfied by God (Ps. 42:1–2). In announcing the arrival of the kingdom in himself, Jesus was invoking this long-anticipated hope, the moment when God's promises would be fulfilled, Israel would be rescued from oppression, evil would be judged, and God would establish a new reign of justice and peace.[15] No longer would divine light be hidden. Now Jesus, the world's true light, would push back the shadows.

However, Jesus defied popular expectations when he entered the world. Born in a stable and raised in the obscurity of Nazareth, he lived under the radar. According to Isaiah 53:2, he looked like a regular guy (he had "no form or majesty that we should look at him"). However, this would change on the banks of the Jordan River when Jesus encountered his cousin, John the Baptist. In that momentous meeting, John fulfilled the prophetic announcement of Israel's restoration: "For this is the one referred to by Isaiah the prophet when he said, 'The voice of one crying in the wilderness, "Prepare the way of the Lord, make his paths straight"'" (Matt. 3:3 NASB).

We may sometimes ask ourselves, why was it important for Jesus to be baptized in water? New Testament scholars have suggested that it was of profound importance to the overarching salvation narrative, that just as Moses's leading Israel through the Red Sea to enter the promised land and the second generation's passing through the water of the Jordan River under Joshua's leadership showcased the restoration of God's people, so did the baptism of John the Baptist.[16] Thus, Christ came to "fulfill all righteousness" (Matt. 3:15) in the sense of coming to set right what Israel and Adam had done wrong, to do faithfully and obediently what previous servants had failed to do.[17] Simply put, "John's baptism was to be the sign of reform that would show that Jesus was committed to letting God's reign dominate his life."[18]

At last, the kingdom had come.[19] According to his righteousness, God sent his Son into the world, a personal embodiment of grace who came to redeem us from the penalty, power, and presence of sin that undermine true life. This dynamic movement of righteousness (or justice, if you prefer) extends from heaven to earth, transforming our mind and affections and reaching further to our friends and loved ones.

God's Saving Activity

Some scholars believe that because the Gospel of Matthew frequently shines a light on the necessity of ethical righteousness (think Pharisees), the focus must be on righteous behavior when we encounter the term "righteousness." Matthew is therefore sometimes cast as the foil of Paul, the champion of salvation by grace. This, however, is a false dichotomy. If Paul the Jew could understand righteousness through the lens of grace, there is no reason that Matthew could not have done the same.[20] Seeing righteousness as a sign of God's saving activity has a long, venerable history in Hebrew Scripture. Consider the following passages:

- "In your righteousness deliver me and rescue me; incline your ear to me, and save me!" (Ps. 71:2)

- "For your name's sake, O Lord, preserve my life! In your righteousness bring my soul out of trouble!" (Ps. 143:11)

This is the first movement of righteousness—a movement in which God manifests his glory by extending his hand of salvation, a justifying grace that turns damned rebels into beloved children.[21] When Matthew the tax collector repented, he experienced God's redeeming righteousness and blessing. So did the prostitutes and those dismissed as "sinners" (Matt. 9:11). Thus Jesus told the religious rulers, "Truly, I say to you, the tax collectors and the prostitutes go into the kingdom of God before you" (Matt. 21:31). Is it any wonder the Jewish leaders sought to arrest him? An alternative kingdom was now encroaching upon their religious economy—indeed, the kingdom of God.[22]

"This blessedness," says Donald Hagner, "is ascribed not to achievers, but to receivers."[23] We must work very hard to resist the natural urge to find something within ourselves that deserves God's favor. From beginning to end we are saved by divine initiative. As the old hymn *Rock of Ages* declares:

Nothing in my hand I bring,
Simply to the cross I cling;
Naked, come to thee for dress,
Helpless, look to thee for grace:
Foul, I to the fountain fly,
Wash me, Savior, or I die.[24]

How else can we explain God's acceptance of cowards such as Abraham and adulterers and murderers such as David (cf.

Rom. 4:1–8)? And of course, how do we explain our own faith? Such acceptance is without "any claim of our own, not even our faith," says Mostert.[25] Justification is "fundamentally about how God deals with humans and the broken, sinful world in which they live. It is, above all, about grace."[26]

We see a beautiful example of such grace in *Les Misérables* when Monseigneur Myriel embraces Jean Valjean. Myriel, you'll recall, is the bishop who invites Valjean (the recently paroled convict) into his home for food, warmth, and a bed. Despite the "highly dangerous" designation on Valjean's papers, Myriel offers unconditional hospitality, declaring, "This is not my house; it is Christ's . . . [therefore] you're welcome."[27] But that night Valjean steals the bishop's valuable silverware. The next morning the police return the stolen goods and set Valjean before the bishop. In what is an obvious case of theft, the merciful Bishop Myriel transforms the situation into a moment of redemption:

> "Ah! There you are!" he exclaimed, looking at Jean Valjean. "I'm glad to see you. Now, look here, I gave you those candlesticks as well, they're silver like the rest and you'll certainly be able to get two hundred francs for them. Why didn't you take them with your forks and spoons?" Jean Valjean's eyes widened, and he stared at the venerable bishop with an expression no human tongue can describe. The bishop [then] went up to him and said quietly, "Don't forget, never forget, you promised to use this money to become an honest man."[28]

How does one explain this? The police were incredulous. Valjean was dumbfounded. Even readers who have heard the story multiple times continue to shake their heads in wonder. Simply put, this is a picture of how God extends righteousness to us.

The righteousness of God begins here, addressing our guilt with mercy and forgiveness. Such grace is the ongoing basis of our relationship with God, but we must be clear that it's not the final goal.[29] In the outworking of salvation, God continues to work his righteousness in and through his children.

A Soul-Renovating Righteousness

In addition to the justifying grace that we encounter before God's throne—the divine favor that declares us to be God's children—we also receive the soul-renovating righteousness that delivers us from the power and pollution of sin by instilling a hunger for God.[30]

If we were to put our finger on a text that conveys the idea of righteousness in us, we can do no better than Matthew 6:33: "But seek first the kingdom of God and his righteousness, and all these things will be added to you." This is the ethical justice that so commonly appears in Matthew's Gospel. Sometimes contrasted by wickedness (see Prov. 10:2), this righteousness comes by the inner working of the Holy Spirit who creates a renewed heart. It is illustrated again in Valjean when he leaves bishop Myriel as a forgiven man, only to momentarily revert to his dishonest ways by stealing a coin from Petit Gervais, a boy who worked as a chimney sweep. Valjean is immediately overwhelmed with guilt, now seeing himself through the lens of the bishop's mercy. Eventually, he breaks down in tears and repents before God. This is what righteousness looks like when it's active within us.

In this vein, Leo Tolstoy famously wrote, "everybody thinks of changing humanity, and nobody thinks of changing himself."[31]

Besides providing a snappy tweet to every motivational speaker and public influencer the world over, Tolstoy reminds us of the importance of inner transformation. In our frenetic lives and outright selfishness, we may easily overlook this calling to spiritual renewal, but it never escapes God's attention. Here are just a couple of examples of where the Old Testament uses the language of righteousness to stress its importance:

- "Thus says the LORD: 'Keep justice, and do righteousness, for soon my salvation will come, and my righteousness be revealed.'" (Isa. 56:1)
- "'I walk in the way of righteousness, in the paths of justice.'" (Prov. 8:20)

The righteousness that makes us children of God also operates within us, renewing our desires. In addition to providing a new heart (Jer. 31:31–34), God imparts a new hunger and thirst, a new appetite. All who are in Christ are a new creation (2 Cor. 5:17).

The renewal of our heart also comes into focus by considering a negative example. Despite God's bountiful provision of manna and quail, the disobedient generation of Israel in the desert was never satisfied. The people sought to control their circumstances instead of relying on the one who promised to be with them (Ex. 3:12). Nevertheless, God provided by giving Israel a daily portion of food and commanded them to not hoard it for the following day. Moses said, "Let no one leave any of it over till morning" (Ex. 16:19 NKJV). Each of them gathered as much as they could eat, but many did not listen to Moses—they left part of the manna until the morning and it bred worms and stank (Ex. 16:20).

This sorry incident may be the background of Matthew's admonition to "not lay up for yourselves treasures on earth, where moth and rust destroy and where thieves break in and steal, but lay up for yourselves treasures in heaven, where neither moth nor rust destroys and where thieves do not break in and steal" (Matt. 6:19–20). Such a hunger, says one commentator, "means to refuse to be satisfied with anything less than God, and this in itself is a fitting definition of the justice that orders the relationship between the Creator and the creature."[32]

To be clear, the insistence on hungering that leads to obedience is not to promote works righteousness. God does not accept us based on our religious behavior (Eph. 2:8–10). Fallen humanity cannot secure even the smallest amount of divine merit by performing good works. Ongoing sin in the life of a believer prevents such achievement, for even the purest and most heroic examples of human virtue remain tainted by the fall and therefore cause us to miss the divine standard. "Unless your righteousness exceeds that of the scribes and Pharisees, you will never enter the kingdom of heaven," Jesus said (Matt. 5:20). And even the most scrupulous saint, who may perhaps feel optimistic looking at the Pharisees' standards, would have to admit defeat after Jesus's next stipulation: "You therefore must be perfect, as your heavenly Father is perfect" (Matt. 5:48). Indeed, the impossibility of attaining divine holiness requires us to embrace Christ, whose perfect righteousness is the sole reason for our hope.

While contending for this gospel of justification by faith alone, the Reformers simultaneously insisted that our faith does not remain alone. Calvin was convinced that "we dream neither of a faith devoid of good works nor of a justification that stands without them,"[33] and this conviction echoes down through generations to the present.[34] United to Christ, we consequently encounter the renovating work of the Spirit, which in turn yields the fruit of righteousness (Gal. 5:22–23).

In this way, Jesus transforms our appetites from the inside out. Such a person, says Martin Luther, "continually works and strives with all his might to promote the general welfare and the proper behavior of everyone and . . . helps to maintain and support this by word and deed, by precept and example."[35] Modern interpreters agree with Luther. For example, Craig Keener suggests that "hungering and thirsting for righteousness probably includes yearning for God's justice, for his vindication of the oppressed."[36] R. T. France understands righteousness as "a synonym for the Christian life"; it is "the ultimate satisfaction of relationship with God unclouded by disobedience."[37] In the same vein, R. Kent Hughes describes righteousness as "a pattern of conformity to God's will."[38]

But the righteousness of God goes even further. It is more than a private affair, more than our individual spirituality. It also extends through us into a Christ-centered movement of social justice.

Justice to the Nations

Earlier we imagined Constantine marching his troops through Italy, crosses emblazoned on shields and armor with the slogan "In this [sign], conquer."[39] This represents one way—an especially popular way—to bring justice to the nations. It turns out, however, that such an approach is out of step with the kingdom.

When Jesus described his kingdom, he consistently emphasized its humble trajectory. His followers are "salt of the earth" and "light of the world" (Matt. 5:13, 14)—servants who enrich others and offer illumination. They express sincere prayers to their heavenly Father so that his will is done "on earth as it is in heaven" (Matt. 6:10). When facing conflict, they first seek to remove the log from their own eye before trying to remove the speck from their brother's eye.

All of this highlights the surprising, countercultural impulse of the kingdom. It's like a mustard seed—so modest and small that it goes unnoticed by humans and birds alike, but in time, sprouting into a bush so large that birds can nest in its branches. Or it is like a merchant who specializes in expensive jewels—one day he finds a pearl of such value that he liquidates his entire estate to buy it. That's the nature of God's kingdom: simultaneously humble and of surpassing value, inconspicuous but growing exponentially beyond our wildest dreams.

Matthew is concerned to show that the righteousness that extends *to* us (justification) and *in* us (sanctification) is intended to reach *through* us to transform the pain and evil of the world.[40] In this way, Matthew stands in the prophetic tradition, connecting the knowledge of God with the actual doing of justice. Consider the following passages from Scripture:

- "But let justice roll down like waters, and righteousness like an ever-flowing stream." (Amos 5:24)
- "[When you share] your bread with the hungry and bring the homeless poor into your house; when you see the naked, to cover him, and not to hide yourself from your own flesh

. . . then shall your light break forth like the dawn, and . . . your righteousness shall go before you." (Isa. 58:7–8)

- "Then the righteous will answer him, saying, 'Lord, when did we see you hungry and feed you, or thirsty and give you drink?' . . . And the King will answer them, 'Truly, I say to you, as you did it to one of the least of these my brothers, you did it to me.'" (Matt. 25:37, 40)

This calling to extend righteousness is difficult. The dizzying complexity of modern life, the ceaseless sniping between partisan factions, and our own contentiousness have undermined the redemptive trajectory of this call. Add to this the typical separation between public life (media, secular institutions, bureaucracies) and our private experience (internal attitudes and perceptions that emerge from personal, familial, and ecclesial identity), and it's not surprising to see the church floundering.

Today, the term "social justice" causes many church members to recoil; they regard it as a variety of socialism, the popular "wokeness" of secular culture on issues such as transgenderism, same-sex marriage, abortion, and poverty.[41] Understandable as this may be, Thaddeus Williams reminds us, "Social justice is not optional for the Christian. (What justice isn't social, for that matter? God designed us as social creatures, made for community, not loners designed to live on a deserted island or staring solo at glowing screens all day)."[42]

In this beatitude, Jesus articulates the full sweep of salvation: *to* us, *in* us, and *through* us. Anything less falls short of our calling. Stated positively, God intends to counterintuitively address the world with the power of the gospel in and through his church.[43]

True Satisfaction

We conclude this chapter with a simple question, "For what do we hunger?"

Since our hearts have been made by and for God, they will never be satisfied until we embrace the full movement of divine righteousness, when we are right with God. We are to ask for righteousness in prayer, experience its power in life's painful trials, extend its hope and healing to others, and continue knocking until God provides his full and final gift of righteousness on the last day.

When this happens, says Jesus, we will be "satisfied" (Matt. 5:6). It's noteworthy that God's blessing is not for those who win the race. It's not for spiritual champions who have arrived. Instead, it's for those who simply hunger and thirst—who recognize their need and desire righteousness, even if they have a long way to go.

Aren't you glad Jesus didn't say, "Blessed are the consistently righteous, for they will be satisfied"? Let's face it; if this were the requirement, all of us would go away empty—every one of us. Thank God it's not the realization of the desire but the desire itself that Christ pronounces his blessing on. It's not the one who attains righteousness, but the one who longs for it.

This is why Jesus endured the indignities of human life (betrayal, arrest, and desertion); why he withstood mockery and slaps in the face from those who ought to have worshiped him; why he was silent before the self-indulgent foolishness of Herod Antipas. It's the reason he endured the crown of thorns, the exposure, the cross. Bonhoeffer thus explains, "Not only do the followers of Jesus renounce their rights, they *renounce their own righteousness* too.

They get no praise for their achievements or sacrifices. They cannot have righteousness except by hungering and thirsting for it."[44]

To be just, then, to long for righteousness, is to refuse to be satisfied by anything less than God. We reject the frivolous, cotton-candy righteousness of consumerism and the images, styles, and behaviors of contemporary culture that purport to validate our self-worth.[45] We likewise reject the righteousness vended by popular Christianity, the kind that promises unlimited health, wealth, and influence. Eating such counterfeit bread leaves us perennially hungry. Instead, genuine wholeness is found in hungering for Jesus Christ, the true bread who came down from the Father.

Herein lies the mystery—that we can be simultaneously hungry *and* satisfied. In Christ, we are both famished and full, laboring and at rest. Martyn Lloyd-Jones captures this counterintuitive turn: "The Christian is one who at one and the same time is hungering and thirsting, and yet he is filled. And the more he is filled, the more he hungers and thirsts. This is the blessedness of the Christian life."[46]

This is God's promise. "Blessed are those who hunger and thirst for righteousness, for they shall be satisfied" (Matt. 5:6).

5

The Face of Mercy

Blessed are the merciful, for they shall receive mercy.

MATTHEW 5:7

OUTLINING THE SQUARE of Saint Petersburg, Russian soldiers stood at attention while convicts assembled nearby in the snow, dressed in light clothing and shivering. Discussion among the prisoners was suddenly interrupted by the command of a general who ordered them to remain silent. Then, a priest carrying a cross stepped forward and declared, "Today you will bear the just decision of your case—follow me."[1]

Among the convicts was a young Fyodor Dostoyevsky (1821–1881), the Russian novelist. At age twenty-eight, he was arrested for belonging to a literary circle considered treasonous by Tsar Nicholas I, whose unjust bureaucracy left many starving for their daily bread.

The priest led the convicts in a procession to a row of gray stakes rising from the ground. The crisp sound of soldiers snapping to attention suddenly echoed through the square. The prisoners were arranged in lines and ordered to remove their caps while their sentences were read. Like the tolling of a funeral bell, the sequential sentencing echoed a common refrain and culminated in a singular conclusion: "The Field Criminal Court has condemned all to death before a firing squad."[2]

The prisoners were given "white peasant blouses and night caps"—their death gowns.[3] The first three men in line were led forward before the firing squad and bound to the stakes. Dostoyevsky, situated in the next row from which the men were selected, looked on in horror. A protracted silence followed. The "suspense of waiting for the firing squad to pull the trigger" lasted about a minute—what one convict described as "terrible, repulsive, [and] frightening."[4] Finally, a horseman arrived with a pre-arranged message from the tsar: instead of execution, Nicholas would "mercifully" commute their sentences to hard labor in Siberia.

The experience remained with Dostoyevsky for the balance of his days. After peering into the great unknown, he suddenly recognized the limits of human reason. In the words of one biographer, "It is from this instant that the primarily secular perspective from which Dostoyevsky had previously viewed human life sinks to the background."[5] Dostoyevsky the theologian was born.

While boarding the convict train to Siberia, a woman gave Dostoyevsky a copy of the only book he was permitted to read in prison—the New Testament. Over the next four years of imprisonment, he would consider the injustices of nineteenth-century Russia in light of Christ's mercy. You might say this was a central concern of Dostoyevsky's life: trying to understand how mercy restores human hearts—indeed, all of creation—to the righteous image of God. The question is just as relevant today.

Our Need for Mercy

It's one of life's truisms. When our eyes are opened to God's kingdom, we begin to recognize injustices in the world that previously didn't occur to us. Hungering for the right ordering of life, we start to feel irritated by the fallen condition of humanity. We get unsettled, or maybe indignant, or perhaps infuriated by wickedness and oppression. Ironically, then, anger becomes the besetting sin of those who crave justice. "Hot indignation seizes me," says the psalmist, "because of the wicked, who forsake your law" (Ps. 119:53).

This indignation may arise from a legitimate source. The more we recognize the true, the good, and the beautiful—the more we hunger for them—the more inclined we will be to get mad at the false, the bad, and the ugly. This is certainly (and rightly) true of anger directed at evil (for example, the tyrant who attacks innocent people, the scam artists who prey on the elderly, or the trusted authority figures who abuse children). However, it also applies to the conflicting motives and misguided behavior of everyday life. The more we walk in the light, the more naturally disturbed we become by moral darkness (Titus 1:15; 1 Pet. 4:1–6).

However, bitter opposition to the darkness—what some today might call the outrage of cancel culture—must never become our normal mode of operation. God calls us to pursue redemption, "for the anger of man does not produce the righteousness of God" (James 1:20). Indeed, "mercy triumphs over judgment" (2:13). This was precisely the message of Dostoyevsky's classic work *The*

Brothers Karamazov, wherein the main character Ivan represents the spiteful punishment and retribution of the world's "justice," a vengeance that "glaringly contrasts with Christ's gospel of all-reconciling and all-forgiving love and the hope of infinite mercy for the sinner who repents."[6]

Unfortunately, we are often blind to our own need for mercy. Consider the character Javert from Victor Hugo's *Les Misérables*, the police inspector whose narrow interpretation of justice became weaponized. In the words of Hugo, "[Javert] had nothing but disdain, aversion, and disgust for all who had once overstepped the bounds of the law."[7] For Javert, the law was a zero-sum game. There were good guys and bad guys, those who kept the law and those who broke the law.

In the end, Javert's greatest strength became his greatest weakness. Driven by a Pharisee-like commitment to the letter of the law, he couldn't overlook the slightest infraction. "Though Javert's toe-the-line mentality is often appropriate and admirable," writes Bob Welch, "it becomes a millstone for him—and society at large—when used without restraint."[8] Javert failed to understand that the law is always a means toward a greater end—that is, toward redemption—not an end unto itself. Aleksandr Solzhenitsyn strikes this note when he writes, "A society which is based on the letter of the law and never reaches any higher is taking very scarce advantage of the high level of human possibilities."[9] Even worse, such a society deprives itself of its most profound need: mercy.

Mercy before God

There are, of course, plenty of positive examples of mercy in *Les Misérables*. For instance, there is Fantine, the self-identified "sinner" whose encounter with mercy delivered her from prostitution—even if not by choice—to become a saint.[10] Before her heart was melted by the mercy of Valjean (as Monsieur Madeleine), Victor Hugo describes her as calloused and coarse, as seen in her response to the dandy who threw snow down her back. Hugo writes,

> The girl roared in rage, turned, bounded like a panther, and rushed at the man, burying her nails in his face, and using the most shocking words usually heard only in the barracks. These insults were thrown out in a voice roughened by brandy, from a hideous mouth minus two front teeth. It was Fantine.[11]

Yet, after a lifetime of humiliation and abandonment—bereft of security or familial love and having lost her teeth, her hair, and her dignity—Fantine is suddenly changed by mercy. The change came when Valjean mercifully intervened. He didn't scold her but instead paid her debts and offered to care for her child, Cosette. It was the righteous and honorable thing for him to do—to offer her the kindness, dignity, and respect that belongs to a divine image bearer. And when she received it, Fantine erupted in praise. Hugo writes, "She felt the fearful darkness of her hatred melt within her and flow away, while an indescribable and ineffable warmth of joy, of confidence, and of love welled up in her heart."[12]

Fantine illustrates the reason why we must never drive a wedge between justice and mercy: they are mutually reinforcing. Rebekah Eklund makes this connection from the teaching of Ambrose of Milan (339–397), who promoted mercy as the necessary outflow of justice, that is, the natural extension of the previous beatitude.[13] Likewise, Augustine (354–430) saw the two in an organic relationship.

He related them by portraying the believer as a hungry beggar at God's door: if you turn away a beggar seeking mercy from your door, God may turn you away from his door.[14]

Admittedly, such an outlook can give the impression that mercy is a religious work required to secure God's favor, a way to merit salvation.[15] But it isn't. Martin Luther famously made clear that our "homemade" righteousness, whether the manifestation of mercy or any other virtue, can never prevail with God.[16] We are sinners, whose "righteous deeds are like a polluted garment" (Isa. 64:6). Nevertheless, Luther insists that mercy is what righteousness looks like in action.[17] In his words, "True righteousness has compassion."[18]

However, we may legitimately ask, "Does God refuse to extend mercy to those who have not been merciful?" After all, James asserts that "judgment is without mercy to one who has shown no mercy" (James 2:13). Such texts suggest a reciprocity or interdependence between our giving of mercy and our receiving of mercy. "Judge not," Jesus says elsewhere in the Sermon on the Mount, "that you be not judged. For with the judgment you pronounce you will be judged" (Matt. 7:1–2). We see the same kind of parallel in the story of the unmerciful slave, whose forgiveness (or the lack thereof) boomerangs back upon himself (Matt. 18:23–35).

Throughout church history, this biblical pattern of reciprocity has raised interesting and provocative questions about salvation, especially among the Protestant Reformers. To many of them, this notion smelled like a divine quid pro quo—the idea that a person would receive divine mercy only after having exercised it himself, which was an error that resembled the sort of meritorious grace defended by the Roman Catholic Church. While Reformers such as Luther and Calvin did not specifically employ Jesus's beatitude on mercy to address the concern, later Protestants would.[19]

Try as we might, we can never secure God's favor through our moral behavior. Martyn Lloyd-Jones writes that "if you and I were to be judged strictly on those terms, it is very certain that not one of us would be forgiven and not one of us would ever seek heaven."[20] Simply put, there's no amount of mercy sinners can exercise to merit salvation. How then should we understand Jesus's words? Thinking with earlier Protestants, Lloyd-Jones suggested that the demonstration of mercy reveals that one already belongs to God.[21] It is the flowering fruit of righteousness that confirms the legitimacy of one's conversion. In the words of John Stott, "[By such mercy] we give evidence of what by God's free grace and gift we already are."[22]

The Cultivation of Mercy

God is full of mercy, and he bestows this fullness on his children. It is no accident that when the Lord of glory appeared to Moses on Mount Sinai and revealed his divine character, he chose to say of himself, "The LORD, the LORD, a God merciful and gracious, slow to anger, and abounding in steadfast love and faithfulness" (Ex. 34:6). It's stunning. Of all the qualities God might have stressed—his holiness, sovereignty, or almighty power—he chose to highlight his tender heart of compassion. As mercy is of central importance to God, so it must be for us. "Be merciful," Jesus says, "even as your Father is merciful" (Luke 6:36).

We are merciful not because God started the process and then leaves us to finish it by the power of our wills. Rather, each step of the way, God melts our self-reliance and feeds our faith until we desire him above all. It is a project of mercy in which Christ continually says, "Come to me, all who labor and are heavy laden, and I will give you rest" (Matt. 11:28). The Lord leads us with "cords of kindness" and with "the bands of love" (Hos. 11:4).

But how exactly do we cultivate our desire for God's mercy? A helpful answer comes from my friend Cecilia Horn, a godly woman and earnest evangelist. I once asked Cece how she cultivates an enthusiasm for sharing the good news. I'll never forget her response. She said, "For many years, I was lost and without hope, like a prisoner living in a dark cave. Then, one day, God called me out from the shadows into the brightness of the noonday sun. At once, I looked heavenward and started blinking, trying to get perspective on the wonder of God's mercy. I continue to blink in grateful amazement that deepens my faith and compels me to share the good news with others."

I find this insight helpful. Remembering our former days of loneliness and shame—when we were alienated from Christ, strangers to the divine promises "having no hope and without God in the world" (Eph. 2:12)—dilates the eyes of our heart and cultivates a deeper appreciation for mercy. With the church we cry, *Kyrie eleison*, "Lord, have mercy!" This is the starting point and foundation of our calling. Before we are led to show mercy to others, we first cultivate it for ourselves.

Mediating Mercy

After receiving God's mercy, we then, in turn, extend it to others. This is easier said than done. We live in a frenetic world, full of time-consuming responsibilities and distractions. It's easy to ignore the needs of our family members who live under the same roof, to say nothing of unseen neighbors and friends. But we are *called* to notice. While passing through Jericho, pressed by the noisy crowd, Jesus looked up to notice a little man watching in a tree. "Zacchaeus, hurry and come down," he said, "for I must stay at your house today" (Luke 19:5). The merciful Jesus *noticed*.

By contrast, though, we often ignore those around us. For example, a seventy-year-old woman named Marinella Beretta was recently found dead in Prestino, near Lake Como in northern Italy.[23] According to an article in *The Guardian*, she was seated at her table in a mummified state when police discovered her remains more than two years after she had died. They stumbled upon this elderly single woman with no relatives after some high winds had risked uprooting the trees in her garden.

Marinella's neighbors, it turns out, had not seen her for at least two-and-a-half years, according to Italian media. She was "loneliness personified," wrote Massimo Gramellini, a journalist covering the story.[24] "Many of us still have memories of the chaotic, branched families of peasant Italy. Instead, the modern family is reduced. . . . People die alone. And we live alone, which is almost worse."[25]

Apparently, the neighbors who had not seen Marinella for all that time simply assumed she had moved during the coronavirus pandemic. The closing words of the article are poignant and convicting: "The mystery of Marinella's invisible life behind the closed gate of her cottage teaches us a terrible lesson. The real sadness is not that the others did not notice her death. It is that they did not realise Marinella Beretta was alive."[26]

Over against this sort of blindness, Jesus shows us how to notice others. "When he saw the crowds, he had compassion for them, because they were harassed and helpless, like sheep without a shepherd" (Matt. 9:36). This is the heartbeat of our beatitude, what Calvin understood as suffering with our neighbor, or what today we might call "empathy."[27] Calvin writes, "We must assume their identity, as it were, so as to be deeply touched by their suffering and moved by love to mourn with them."[28] Jeremiah Burroughs further adds, "Mercy causes one to put himself into the same state, to be in bonds with those that are in bonds, and to weep with those that weep."[29]

The Fruit of Mercy

Manifesting God's mercy will produce not a small trickle but a massive deluge of forgiveness. Peter once asked Jesus, "Lord, how often will my brother sin against me, and I forgive him? As many as seven times?" (Matt. 18:22). Peter was proud of his far-reaching forgiveness, having exceeded the accepted norm.[30] However, Jesus famously responded, "I do not say to you seven times, but seventy-seven times" (Matt. 18:22). The lavish extent of divine mercy almost seems irresponsible. "Forgiveness is reckless," says Simeon Tugwell. "It squanders itself upon rogues who have no intention of improving themselves. All it asks for is that it be received. The only unforgivable sin is the sin against forgiveness, the sin which directly and immediately refuses forgiveness."[31]

During my years as a pastor, I have witnessed a range of merciless situations. In this context, people often confess that they lack the ability to forgive others: the man who was abused as a child or the wife of an alcoholic husband. They are undoubtedly right—apart from Jesus. Because God alone can fully heal our wounds and revive the dead, we need to acquire his heart if we are to forgive others. In view of this, Jesus said, "Father, forgive them, for they know not what they do" (Luke 23:34). Should we say anything less?

In this way, forgiveness is not an example of mere benevolence; it is an act of faith and hope. By extending forgiveness to others, we demonstrate our belief that Christ will return and mercifully set all things right. Our salvation enables us to face the most grievous forms of evil with hope. "Where sin increased," says Paul, "grace abounded all the more" (Rom. 5:20). Later in the same epistle, Paul says, "For I consider that the sufferings of this present time are not worth comparing with the glory that is to be revealed to us" (Rom. 8:18).

We sometimes catch a glimpse of that glory in the unlikeliest of places. Corrie ten Boom tells the story of meeting a former SS officer from the Ravensbrück concentration camp—a man who had stood guard at the shower room—after she had spoken at a church in Munich in 1947. She writes:

> He was the first of our actual jailers that I had seen since that time. . . . He came up to me as the church was emptying, beaming and bowing. "How grateful I am for your message, *Fraulein*," he said. "To think that, as you say, He has washed my sins away!" His hand was thrust out to shake mine. And I, who had preached so often to the people in Bloemendaal the need to forgive, kept my hand at my side. Even as the angry, vengeful thoughts boiled through me, I saw the sin of them. . . . *Lord Jesus*, I prayed, *forgive me and help me to forgive him.* I tried to smile, I struggled to raise my hand. I could not. And so again I breathed a silent prayer. *Jesus, I cannot forgive him. Give Your*

forgiveness. As I took his hand the most incredible thing happened. From my shoulder along my arm and through my hand, a current seemed to pass from me to him, while into my heart sprang a love for this stranger that almost overwhelmed me.[32]

In that moment Corrie ten Boom, a middle-aged survivor of Nazi terror, committed an act not of hateful revenge, but of faith and hope. Her decision was truly extraordinary. In so doing, she pointed to—and in a small but significant way tasted—the already-but-not-yet kingdom of Christ. This is the fruit of mercy.

The Transforming Power of Mercy

Iconography and traditional Christian art often depict pious-looking, haloed saints wearing luminescent garments and surrounded by fiery angels. But how many of these saints were in fact murderers like Paul, adulterers like David, or otherwise worldly people like Augustine whose stubbornness required decades of tears and intercessory prayer on the part of his mother—sinners who became great saints?

It's interesting to consider how these members of the great cloud of witnesses would be treated today. Would they be summarily canceled for their preconversion lives? In a time when binding verdicts are pronounced before evidence is considered—where accusations are tantamount to guilt—would these saints even be considered as objects of mercy? Does the church today have the capacity to recognize the transforming power of God's compassion—the salvation that separates sin from someone as far as the east is from the west? In other words, can we surround sinners with genuine love to the extent that we value, honor, and serve them?

"Mercy," says Sinclair Ferguson, "is getting down on your hands and knees and doing something to restore dignity to someone whose life has been broken by sin."[33]

I once had the privilege of observing such compassion in action. When my friend David returned on furlough from missionary service in Europe, he called to ask whether he and his wife Margaret could visit our home in the suburbs.[34] In earlier years, David had been an intern and by now was a significant church leader in his country. On several occasions we had served together overseas, and we never missed an opportunity to enjoy fellowship when he was back in the States.

But I could tell from David's voice that something was wrong. Upon arriving, he asked if we could go for a walk, leaving Margaret with my wife, Angela. As soon as we stepped out of the door, David began to confess marital infidelity. As we walked, he said that he had not yet told Margaret but realized his need to do so. We walked together for about twenty minutes, agreeing that when we returned to my house, he would confess.

I felt like I was like watching a train wreck in slow motion—with loved ones sitting in the train. Margaret listened attentively as David poured out the lurid details of his sin. I watched her eyes begin to fill with tears as her life collapsed before her. Then, after about ten minutes of David's monologue, there was silence. Poor Margaret. The ever-faithful pastor's wife, who was entirely devoted to her husband and to their ministry, was dealt the deepest blow imaginable. I imagined demons cackling with glee as the shadows of shame and condemnation encircled them.

But then, Margaret began to speak. She lifted her chin resolutely, face shining like an angel, and announced, "I am committed to

Christ. I am committed to our family. And therefore, I am committed to you, David." With each word, the light of heaven shone more brightly, and the shadows of condemnation rolled back. There was, of course, a journey of restoration and healing before them. But the decisive step—her statement of mercy—enabled them to escape the shadows and begin the journey together.

Every time we extend mercy, forgiveness, and compassion in the name of Christ—a love that pardons another of his guilt—we showcase his coming reign, a kingdom blessing that we enjoy here on earth as it is in heaven.

"Blessed are the merciful, for they shall receive mercy" (Matt. 5:7).

Seeing God

Blessed are the pure in heart, for they shall see God.
MATTHEW 5:8

IN HER BOOK TITLED *Her Heart Can See: The Life and Hymns of Fanny J. Crosby*, historian Edith Blumhofer offers an intimate look at the hymn writer's faith. You may know something of Crosby's legacy. After losing her sight during infancy through a doctor's negligence, she went on to compose over nine thousand hymns, including such classics as "Blessed Assurance," "Jesus, Keep Me Near the Cross," and "I Am Thine, O Lord."

Crosby's voluminous output was indebted to her extraordinary mind. According to one of her collaborators, Hugh Main, she could dictate two hymns simultaneously, alternating between the lines of each poem and keeping two secretaries busy.[1] This, however, was only part of her ministry. For over two decades, she personally visited the marginalized and downtrodden of society at Manhattan's rescue missions.[2] For many of these occasions she wrote and presented hymns that stressed God's gracious renewal of the heart. The best known of these is perhaps "Rescue the Perishing." One stanza reads:

Down in the human heart,
Crushed by the tempter,
Feelings lie buried that grace can restore;
Touched by a loving heart, wakened by kindness,
Chords that were broken will vibrate once more.[3]

Crosby was also an evangelist who urged Christians to give themselves fully to proclaiming the gospel. In doing so, she often motivated her listeners by pointing to the end of life when believers encounter Christ face-to-face. For example, in her song "Saved by Grace" she writes:

Some day the silver cord will break,
And I no more as now shall sing;
But oh, the joy when I shall wake
Within the palace of the King!

And I shall see Him face to face,
And tell the story—saved by grace.[4]

Through the centuries, the church has described this culminating hope with the language of beatific vision (1 Cor. 13:12). Bonaventure's *Journey of the Mind to God*, Dante's *Divine Comedy*, and, of course, Bunyan's portrait of Christian reaching the

Celestial City in *The Pilgrim's Progress* all hit this note. In view of this tradition, we shall consider how God transforms our hearts in the present to prepare us for that great day.

The Essence of the Heart

Before we consider Jesus's blessing upon the pure in heart, we should consider what Scripture means by the word "heart." In modern parlance, this often denotes the soppy sentimentalism of a Hallmark card—the emotional core of our being that gives way to feelings such as love or sorrow. Thus, we often distinguish "heart" from "intellect," the former centering on emotion while the latter relating to the mind.

However, in the language and logic of Scripture, this is not so. The heart is the locus of thought, the place where vision is developed.[5] For example, the psalmist writes, "[I] remembered my songs in the night. My heart mused and my spirit asked" (Ps. 77:6 NIV). On the other hand, Genesis tells us that prior to the flood, God noted "how great the wickedness of the human race had become, and that every inclination of the thoughts of the human heart was only evil all the time" (Gen. 6:5 NIV).[6]

When the Bible conveys internal dialogue, whether it is a prayer to God or personal reflection, it uses the idiom of the heart. Hannah prayed to God "in her heart" (1 Sam. 1:13), and in Ecclesiastes the Teacher's mental processes are reported as something he "said in [his] heart" (Eccl. 2:1, 15). Indeed, as Mary witnessed the events associated with the birth of her son Jesus, she "pondered them in her heart" (Luke 2:19 NIV).

But it goes even deeper. Matthew connects "heart" with the act of seeing to describe the way God examines our inner attitudes, evaluates our motives, and observes our private behavior. Jesus said, "But I say to you that everyone who looks at a woman with lustful intent has already committed adultery with her in his heart" (Matt. 5:28). Such heart motivations and intentions are the focal point of the kingdom.

In accordance with this, Jesus then exhorts his disciples, "Be perfect, therefore, as your heavenly Father is perfect" (Matt. 5:48 NIV). "Perfect" here may also be translated "mature" or "whole," meaning loving with sincerity. It's not so much an unachievable ideal as a calling for his disciples to pursue divine purity. Jesus stated this negatively when he said a few verses later, "Beware of practicing your righteousness before other people in order to be seen by them, for then you will have no reward from your Father who is in heaven" (Matt. 6:1).

Such wholeness (or purity) is the leading edge of our identity and calling. "The aim of our charge," says Paul, "is love that issues from a pure heart and a good conscience and a sincere faith" (1 Tim. 1:5). This is precisely where the Jewish leaders of Jesus's day failed. Not only did they try to impress their contemporaries through religious theater, but they also "entertain[ed] evil thoughts in [thei]r hearts" while doing so (Matt. 9:4 NIV). Such duplicity is damning, as Jesus indicates later in Matthew's Gospel when he says, "Woe to you, scribes and Pharisees, hypocrites! For you clean the outside of the cup and the plate, but inside they are full of greed and self-indulgence. You blind Pharisee! First clean the inside of the cup and the plate, that the outside also may be clean" (Matt. 23:25–26).

Of course, the problem was not limited to Pharisees. Describing humanity, Jesus says, "For out of the heart come evil thoughts, murder, adultery, sexual immorality, theft, false witness, slander" (Matt. 15:19). And then, the same heart audaciously expresses allegiance to God (Matt. 22:37). In John Bunyan's *Pilgrim's Progress*, this is illustrated by Mr. Facing Both-Ways,[7] the ridiculous character of contradictions who one writer describes as, "the fellow with one eye on heaven and one on earth—who sincerely preaches one thing and sincerely does another, and from the intensity of his unreality, is unable to see or feel contradiction."[8] Of this embarrassing duplicity James simply says, "These things ought not to be so" (James 3:10).

A Sick and Inward-Facing Heart

Given the compromised nature of our heart, hypocrisy is a problem. "For I do not do the good I want," says Paul, "but the evil I do not want is what I keep on doing" (Rom. 7:19). Despite his best attempts, the apostle missed the mark. This happens, says Paul, because of indwelling sin, for the human heart is fundamentally compromised (Jer. 17:9). Ivan Turgenev, the Russian novelist, said it well: "I do not know what the heart of a bad man is like. But I do know what the heart of a good man is like. And it is terrible."[9]

The trouble is that the sinful heart is turned in toward itself and away from God. This turn results in falsehood and pride, says Augustine, which lead into further isolation and conflict.[10] Years later, Martin Luther built on this assessment, explaining that

our nature is so curved in upon itself at its deepest levels that it not only bends the best gifts of God toward itself in order to enjoy them . . . [and thus] "uses" God in order to obtain them, but it does not even know that, in this wicked, twisted, crooked way, it seeks everything, including God, only for itself.[11]

This portrait agrees with Scripture in identifying the heart as the core problem. Even our most humble and altruistic deeds—our service to others and pursuit of the common good—inevitably become occasions for pride. Our pretensions to purity often conceal a secret sin beneath the surface. "There is something in humility," writes the bishop of Hippo, "which, strangely enough, exalts the heart, and something in pride which debases it."[12] In other words our sinful heart is a black hole that draws into its vortex our most admirable attempts at purity, a gravity that drags us away from God into deeper levels of darkness.

This internal heartbeat is illustrated by the Greek myth of Narcissus, the charming young man whose pride led him to dismiss the advances of the nymphs who sought his attention. One day, a maiden who Narcissus rejected prayed that the prideful youth would himself experience unrequited love. Nemesis, the goddess of righteous anger, answered the maiden's request by causing Narcissus to fall in love with himself to the exclusion of all else. The next day, when Narcissus looked at his reflection in a pool of clear water, he became so entranced that he could not look away. At once, he lost interest in everything else, including food and sleep. In that place of beatific terror, he pined away and eventually died. While Charon, the ferryman of death, transported him across the river to Hades, Narcissus could not resist leaning over the edge of the boat to see his face one last time.

So, we're confronted by the question: Who or what has the power to break our self-obsessed trance, to cleanse the sinful heart? Or in Paul's words, "Who will deliver me from this body of death?" (Rom. 7:24).

God's Solution: A New Heart

From the beginning of his *Confessions*, Augustine is driving at this point. Speaking to God, he says: "You have made us for yourself, and our heart is restless until it rests in you."[13] It's noteworthy that here Augustine uses the singular "heart" and not plural "hearts," as is often quoted ("our hearts are restless"). The singular suggests that humanity shares a common heart and thus the same need—for our emptiness to be filled with God's purifying presence. According to Augustine, this is precisely what God's Spirit accomplishes through Scripture, a transformation that breaks our terminal trance.[14]

Such transformation sometimes comes in unexpected moments. My own restless heart was awakened at the age of nineteen after five weeks into a hospital stay with meningitis. I began to ask new questions. Why was I alive? Is there really a God, and, if so, does he care about me? With each day, the number of questions grew into a resolution to find answers.[15] By the time the young nurse rolled my wheelchair through the hospital exit, my spiritual quest was underway.

My first step was to pursue transcendental meditation under the Maharishi Mahesh Yogi. After a few months of making unusual noises in a lotus position, I understood why the Beatles became disenchanted with Mr. Yogi's method. The apex of this outlandish season of searching was a fire walk at New York's Jacob Javits Center, where more than a thousand people heard motivational speaker Tony Robbins. After three hours of his encouraging affirmations, our massive herd shuffled outside to the parking lot where we encountered long stretches of burning coals and embers. According to Robbins, the experience was designed to be a metaphor for overcoming our fears and improving life. Never had a metaphor looked so harmful.

When the lady ahead of me proceeded to walk across the twelve-foot path of fire, I inhaled deeply. Tony Robbins's wife (who happened to be facilitating my line) put her hand on my shoulder and said, "You can do this!" I noticed that she was wearing shoes and was at least twenty inches from the nearest flaming briquet; nevertheless, I stepped forward and moved as quickly as my trembling legs could carry me. I don't know how it worked; all I can say is that I walked across the fire without getting burned. Despite the thrill, however, the longing of my heart persisted.

As the spiritual quest unfolded, I eventually befriended a Christian. In time, she invited me to visit her church on a Wednesday night. Naturally disposed to decline, I listened as the word proceeded from my mouth in response to her invitation. I, more than anyone, was surprised by what I heard: "Yes."

With a mixture of humiliation and curiosity I entered the doors of Faith Church and sat in the rear pew. My friend eventually arrived and sat beside me. After forty minutes of choruses that seemed familiar to everyone but me, the senior pastor entered the pulpit. With a style that combined Al Pacino and a young Billy Graham, he exclaimed:

Everyone on earth faces the same fundamental choice. Will we continue to live in restlessness of soul, isolated from God? Or will we rest in the one who died for our sins and rose victoriously from the grave? The former person dies in a never-ending state of alienation; the latter enjoys a new heart with which we cry out "*Abba*, Father."

I don't know how to properly describe what came next, except that something within me changed. Like Augustine, Pascal, Luther, Newton, and countless others, this convert's life was profoundly changed. To this day, I don't have a better way to describe it than with the words of John Newton:

Amazing grace (how sweet the sound)
that saved a wretch like me!
I once was lost, but now am found,
was blind, but now I see.[16]

That was the turning point. Through the atoning death and triumphant resurrection of Christ, my calloused heart was suddenly enlivened and enabled to behold the "light of the knowledge of the glory of God in the face of Jesus Christ" (2 Cor. 4:6).

Seeing Christ

This experience—the movement from blindness to spiritual sight—is the way of salvation. Addressing his congregation in Hippo, Augustine preached, "Our whole business in this life is to restore to health the eye of the heart whereby God may be seen."[17] This is a seeing that surpasses sight. It is the vision of God.[18] The logic is simple. Since nothing in all creation is greater than God, seeing him is the greatest possible joy, so much so that "when we pass from this world and see the face of Christ, the joy of that first split second will transcend all the accumulated joys of life."[19]

Unfortunately, in our fallen condition, this is not our natural inclination. Since the fall, we prefer to hide in the shadows. Embarrassed, ashamed, and afraid, we hide from God's presence, either by crawling into a fetal position (literally or figuratively) or trying to overcome our fear with a display of arrogance and bluster. Haunted by the failures of our hearts, we descend into the abyss of shame. Instead of resting in God's provision of purity, we spiral downward into ever-deepening layers of alienation and reproach. But then, just as we begin to lose hope, the Lord meets us in the valley. What John Newton writes here of his conversion also applies to the Christian experience of pursuing divine purity:

In evil long I took delight,
Unawed by shame or fear,
Till a new object struck my sight.
And stopped my wild career.[20]

What was the object of his sight that transferred him from darkness to light? What could possibly purify the heart of this depraved slave trader? He tells us:

I saw One hanging on a tree,
In agonies and blood,
Who fixed His languid eyes on me,
As near the Cross I stood.[21]

The vision of the crucified Savior struck him pure. The filthy sailor with the blood of innocent women and children on his hands suddenly became a holy man in relation to God, and we sing his hymns to this day. Newton beheld the glory of God in the loving face of Jesus Christ, a vision that drove him into deeper dimensions of purity. As Paul writes, "And we all, with unveiled face, beholding the glory of the Lord, are being transformed into the same image from one degree of glory to another. For this comes from the Lord who is the Spirit" (2 Cor. 3:18).

That is precisely where God meets us—in the valley of humiliation. He dwells among us, gradually turning our night into day. In our brokenness and pain, he reveals his loveliness alongside our ugliness. He enables us to behold his presence, even amid deplorable circumstances. Darkness may be our only companion, but the indwelling Spirit nevertheless remains with us, providing wisdom that is "first pure, then peaceable, gentle, open to reason, full of mercy and good fruits" (James 3:17).

This is, once again, the counterintuitive pattern of the kingdom. A Spirit-empowered life does not mean believers are untouched by evil, levitating above the ground with an angelic purity or a syrupy sensation. True life, rather, comes when we look at the man upon the cross, recognizing that what we see is the greatness, power, glory, victory, and majesty of God (1 Chron. 29:11).

Walking with a Limp

So, how do we order our lives in a way that upholds this Christ-centered vision? Let me introduce you to a man named Jake Isaacson. You might say Jake was a little spoiled by his parents. Surrounded by wealth and privilege, he was permitted to hang around the house while his hardworking brother labored outside.

Jake couldn't compete with his older brother in sports, but Jake was smart—maybe too smart. He was also a smooth talker.

In fact, one day he swindled his brother out of a fortune. At an opportune moment, he wrote down an agreement on the back of an envelope and handed his brother a pen. When it was done, Jake smirked at his impetuous brother. "You can keep the pen," he said.

Later, when big brother realized what Jake had done, he wanted to kill him. And he would have done so, if not for their mom, who sent Jake out of the house by night with little more than the clothes on his back. He fled to another city, where no one knew him, and had to start over.

But Jake, a natural schemer, wasn't going to give up so easily. Bernie Madoff, the great fraudster and financier, was his mentor. Shady deals, like the one he had made with his impulsive brother, seemed to follow him. Along the way, Jake met a beautiful young woman, married her, and had children; but he eventually offended his father-in-law. In time, this conflict led him to put his wife and kids in the family SUV and all their stuff into a U-Haul—a very big U-Haul—and hit the highway.

Jake decided their best bet was to return to his hometown and start over again. Surely his brother had cooled off by now. So, Jake called home to see if it was safe. No one answered, so he left a voicemail and stepped on the gas. But as he got closer to the destination, his cell phone rang. It was his brother.

"I hear you're coming home," his older brother said. "I'll be waiting."

Jake swallowed hard.

This story, of course, is a modern retelling of a familiar narrative in the Bible. The conclusion is found in Genesis 32. Sending his family and servants before him with gifts for his older brother Esau, "Jacob was left alone" (32:24). And then came a stranger to wrestle with him. They wrestled "until the breaking of the day" (v. 24). When the man saw that he did not prevail against Jacob, he touched his hip socket and Jacob's hip was put out of joint. Then the man said, "Let me go, for the day has broken" (v. 26). Jacob, however, would not release his grip, only now he was not fighting but holding on like a man who was drowning. "I will not let you go unless you bless me," he exclaimed (v. 26).

Poet Luci Shaw conveys Jacob's desire with these words from "With Jacob":

Inexorably I cry
as I wrestle
for the blessing
thirsty, straining
for the joining
till my desert throat
runs dry.
I must risk
the shrunken sinew
and the laming
of his naming
till I find
my final quenching
in the hollow
of the thigh.[22]

Jacob's restless cry from his heart is our cry. It reflects a craving for nothing less than God. It is a cry for divine communion that can be satisfied only as our spiritual blindness is replaced with spiritual sight. As the English Puritan William Ames says, "Our communion with God is our formal blessedness and is commonly called the vision of God and the beatific vision."[23] This, according to Ames, does not consist in seeing with our eyes or speculating with our minds. It comes from pure grace in which we know, trust, and enjoy Christ.

Such restful communion, however, comes not to the complacent or presumptuous. Paul says, "I do not run aimlessly; I do not box as one beating the air. But I discipline my body and keep it under control, lest after preaching to others I myself should be disqualified" (1 Cor. 9:26–27). Sometimes it requires intense effort—like a wrestling match that leaves you limping. In what remains, then, we will consider an opposition and obstacle to this vision, that is, an everyday barrier that hinders us from beholding God.

The Purifying Vision of God

There are few portions of Scripture that offer a more inspiring vision of God than the Sermon on the Mount. After leading us to consider our prized "treasures" (Matt. 6:19–21)—the things we value most—Jesus urges us to examine the obstacles to our spiritual sight. He says, "The eye is the lamp of the body. So, if your eye is healthy, your whole body will be full of light, but if your eye is bad, your whole body will be full of darkness. If then the light in you is darkness, how great is the darkness!" (Matt. 6:22–23). This statement requires a bit of explanation.

Today we understand the eye to be an organ that receives light so we can see. In the ancient world, however, people understood the eye to function like the sun: it emanated light that arose from one's heart. If the heart was pure, the light shining through the eye would reflect that purity. But if the heart was evil, the eye would mirror that wickedness (hence the term, "evil eye"). And, of course, it also works the other way around. The good or evil things we set our attention on inevitably influence our heart. This integral connection between the eye and the heart is Jesus's central point; Michael Crosby explains, "If one is absorbed in the experience of God's reign, one's whole person will be endowed with light's perfection."[24]

This is our calling—as those who once lived in darkness, to walk as "children of light" (Eph. 5:8). To do so, the New Testament cautions us to avoid specific temptations and threatening distractions. One such example is to resist the mundane cares of the world. Jesus said, "Therefore I tell you, do not be anxious about your life, what you will eat or what you will drink, nor about your body, what you will put on. Is not life more than food, and the body more than clothing?" (Matt. 6:25). Such cares choke God's word from flourishing in our heart and prevent us from seeing him (Matt. 13:22).

In a culture of nonstop advertising aimed at piquing our discontent and fear, marketing that makes us semineurotic about what we eat and the clothing we wear, our hearts are restless, always trying to extend ourselves with finite goods to bolster our identity. We become consumed with our place in society, developing a hyperawareness toward other people that sees them as big and God as small—that values human interaction, and not divine worship, as ultimate.

So, this beatitude is a gracious reminder that the focus of our sight is inextricably linked with the focus of our heart. Those who look to the one who was raised on the tree for their justification are saved, but they are not saved to continue in their lives of impurity. Rather, they are saved from impurity to life anew, a gradual and messy process (from our point of view) that increasingly cherishes Christ over the vain things that charm us most. As Philip Yancey noted, "The proof of spiritual maturity is not how pure you are but awareness of your impurity."[25] That very awareness opens the door to purity and to seeing God.

Those who are seeking purity are also seeking the Lord, and, like a thirsty man in the desert, will find both and quench their thirst forever. Those who clear their minds of the impure clutter of this world "will behold the king in his beauty; they will see a land that stretches afar" (Isa. 33:17).

"Blessed are the pure in heart, for they shall see God" (Matt. 5:8).

7

Peace Be with You

*Blessed are the peacemakers, for they
shall be called sons of God.*

MATTHEW 5:9

"THE CHILD HAS SEVERE HEMOPHILIA," the doctor said.
Looking up at me from the crib with charming brown eyes lay
a beautiful baby boy. A "severe" hemophiliac? My son? Emotions swirled. "Are you sure?" I asked, feeling pathetic. "Yes," he
responded.

Much of life happens before we're ready—especially the hard
stuff. Our hearts race and our minds search for meaning, but some
circumstances resist explanation. So it was for me on that day,
surrounded by the beeping sounds of the neonatal unit. Powerless,
I simply stood and watched.

Thus our parenting journey began. The path of fear and anxiety
was punctuated by moments of calm intimacy with God. Often

feeling bewildered and broken, I reflected on the Lord's promise to provide peace that "surpasses all understanding" (Phil. 4:7), needing it for myself but also wanting to showcase it for onlookers—to doctors, nurses, neighbors, and friends. The desire of my heart was to model Jesus's words and let my "light shine before others" (Matt. 5:16).

In a world where peace seems to be in increasingly short supply, how do we live in peace as Paul emphatically implores his readers to in 2 Corinthians 13:11? Harder yet, how do we live that out even further by becoming the peacemakers Jesus commands us to be?

The Need for Peace

We must first address the great swirl of conflict within ourselves— our selfishness, greed, lust, and every other impulse that keeps us from peace or shalom. Let's be clear, there is no possibility of peace or peacemaking if we refuse to confront ourselves and find God's peace through repentance and faith. We'll never be able to mediate peace to others without honestly and courageously doing business with our own hearts.[1]

Contrary to popular opinion, peacemaking is not simply being nice or kind toward others. Nor can it be reduced to extinguishing flames of hostility, important as that is. It is, rather, God's divine plan for community living in which Christ fills our hearts and then, by extension, permeates the world. It is the shalom Cornelius Plantinga Jr. describes when he says lambs will snuggle up to lions and humans will be knit together by divine love.[2] This is the full-orbed peace of the kingdom of God, of people who are "reconciled to God, know God is for peace, and seek reconciliation instead of strife and war."[3]

Unfortunately, our world is anything but peaceful. In 2022, we watched the horrifying images of Russian forces dropping bombs on Ukrainian cities. We saw artillery shells destroying residential neighborhoods, a tank crushing a family in their car, a maternity hospital destroyed, and apartment complexes reduced to rubble. Countless numbers of refugees, including unaccompanied children, walked untold miles into neighboring Poland with tears running down their cheeks.

Perhaps a good place to start is with a basic observation: the way God extends peace resembles the way he imparts justice—to us, in us, and through us. As Paul explains, God offers peace *to* the justified "through our Lord Jesus Christ" (Rom. 5:1). It is the setting of our minds on the Spirit that results in deep dimensions of peace *within* (Rom. 8:6). And finally, it is our calling to let God's peace flow *through* us by pursuing "what makes for peace and for mutual upbuilding" (Rom. 14:19). This sequence matters because we can't offer what we don't already possess. Peace with God leads to peace in ourselves and eventually to peace in our communities.

"Only the person at peace with God," writes Rebekah Eklund, "can treat her fellow humans peaceably, or can broker peace between his neighbors."[4] She explains, "The theme that peacemakers must first make peace in their own hearts occurs repeatedly among patristic thinkers (including Gregory of Nyssa, Clement of Alexandria, Jerome, and Ambrose of Milan) as well as Reformation-era writers (Erasmus, Luther)."[5] It begins with an attitude before it becomes an action.

In this way, peacemakers illustrate the full sweep of our Christian calling—"wholeness and harmony rather than strife and discord in all aspects of life."[6] That such peace is needed in the world is painfully obvious, for what Thomas Watson wrote in the seventeenth century is equally true today: "Satan kindles the fire of contention in men's hearts and then stands and warms himself at the fire."[7]

When we search for the kindling wood of Satan's fire, we usually find it in the subterranean levels of our heart, particularly in smoldering fears and apprehensions that question the Father's goodness. I now realize this is what occurred to me in the months following my son's diagnosis. When the clouds of fear and consternation gathered, I became like Job, unable to see the Lord through the encircling gloom. I could hardly access peace for myself, much less offer it to others. Herein lies the devil's strategy: distract us with fear, undermine our faith, and derail the enterprise of peacemaking.

The Outcome of Surrendering Peace

Today, after twenty years of pastoral ministry, serving more than a few troubled and distracted people even while attempting to subdue my own challenges, I understand the problem better. It comes down to our heart—our sinful, impulsive, and unpredictable heart. According to James, the human heart is driven by passions that produce quarrels and fights. We desire things but do not get them, which stimulates aggression, covetousness, and even murder (James 4:1–2). This, it turns out, is again the biggest obstacle to peacemaking—ourselves.

What makes matters worse is that our human passions are seldom grounded in reality. Satan enjoys fanning our emotions into flame by instilling fear and dread, often by conjuring worst-case scenarios. In the words of Uncle Screwtape, the senior demon of

C. S. Lewis's tale, "There is nothing like suspense and anxiety for barricading a human's mind against [God]."[8] It's a smokescreen, intended to disorient and deceive. I resonate with the way French philosopher Michel de Montaigne is said to have put it: "My life has been full of terrible misfortunes, most of which never happened."[9] Like a set of dominos falling in the wrong direction, the enemy begins with some fear or anxiety, which leads to unbelief and results in the utter evacuation of peace.

Maybe you can relate. Very often, it is merely the fearful *thought* of catastrophe that consumes us: the dread of illness, concern for one's children, loneliness, financial misfortune, anxiety about old age, unpleasant memories that haunt us, or fear that we will arise one morning and discover the ladder we've so vigorously climbed has been leaning against the wrong wall. In short, we're often plagued by a persistent current of anxiety and unbelief that causes Christ and his eternal purposes to fade from view.

Such anxiety has a destabilizing effect on peacemaking. The anxious person, says James, has a divided mind that makes him unstable "in all his ways" (James 1:8). We become emotionally unstable with divided affections, intellectually unstable with divided thoughts, and relationally unstable with divided loyalty and conviction. Being unstable in every dimension of life causes us to be bereft of peace—both internally and externally—for anxiety causes simple things to be hard and hard things to be agonizing.

We recognize, of course, that some people struggle more than others, but we are all affected. As soon as Adam and Eve listened and acted on Satan's deception, insecurity began to grip their souls. Their fearful imagination suddenly created distorted and perverse conceptions of God. The loving Father now appeared more like a cruel adversary. Sin dominated and gave birth to delusional thinking (Jer. 17:9; Rom. 1:18–21; 2 Cor. 10:5) and peacemaking became scarce. With fruit juice on their lips and a malevolent conception of God in their minds, the first couple turned from the Lord. Fleeing his presence, they pitched their tent in the shadowlands, a place of shame and further alienation.

With this dark and godless outlook, some have become megalomaniacs who actively oppose peace: Nero, Hitler, Stalin, Mao Zedong, Pol Pot. Their cruelty was fueled by fear—hatred of the Jews, Slavs, Gypsies, capitalism, and Christians, a phobia that stirred up division and strife.

On the other side of the godless spectrum are the snowflakes who actively sidestep peace and peacemaking. The darkness of Adam's shadow leads these people to figuratively crawl into a fetal position and suck their thumbs. They are afraid of criticism, rejection, and failure, relinquishing hope that they can overcome life's shadows. They refuse to subdue their fleshly passions and inner conflicts, preferring instead to complain about how they've been wronged. They are victims, so consumed by bitterness that they cannot look beyond their grievances and therefore never rise to the challenge of peacemaking.

The real estate between these extremes is where most people live. We have moments of anxiety and irritability—maybe for days, weeks, or a season—but thank God it does not last forever. Deeper and more basic than this inner turmoil is our identity as sons and daughters of God in union with Christ, indwelt by the Holy Spirit. Such indwelling subdues our hearts and leads us inexorably, if not haltingly, toward peace. It won't surprise you, though, to learn that this too comes in a counterintuitive fashion.

The New Testament's Ironic Power

You might say that the West has experienced a perfect storm in recent years: a swirl of social isolation due to viruses, ferocious election cycles, nonstop political combat, and cold-blooded warfare in Europe. These traumatic factors and others have undermined peace in our world today. In my community, for example, we have seen a drastic escalation in hospitalizations and interventions, along with depression, chemical dependence, abuse, suicidal ideation, and self-harm. The most prevalent symptom, though, is not so obvious. It's the low-level hum that hides in the corners of our minds, the feeling of discouragement or melancholy that imagines God and his redemptive promises to be irrelevant and distant.

The natural human response to such melancholy is to counteract it with positivity. This, again, is how Robert Schuller famously applied the Beatitudes in his book *The Be (Happy) Attitudes* as a tool to stimulate happiness. In sum, one is to apply the animating power of inner joy and peace to become a peacemaker. Schuller writes, "Yes, all of us can be peacemakers—wherever we are. There may be tension inside of you, in your home, or in your place of business. But you can resolve this tension if you give it all you've got."[10]

Part of this proposal, of course, is correct. As we've suggested, we must first lay hold of God's peace ourselves before we can share it with others. And to be sure, Paul exhorts believers to rejoice in all things. Such rejoicing, however, does not come through self-will but is always set in the context of Jesus's death and resurrection (Phil. 2:17; 4:10–13), a downward movement of brokenness and sacrifice that yields one's will for the sake of the other.

In theological terms, it's the so-called "upsilon vector"—an admittedly abstruse-sounding term that has exceedingly practical importance for Christian living.[11]

"Upsilon" is a Greek letter that looks like the English capital U.[12] Its contours represent the trajectory of Jesus's earthly ministry in terms of his descent into apparent defeat (suffering and dying on the cross) before ascending three days later in a triumphant resurrection.[13] It is the counterintuitive pattern of Christian experience that my seminary professor Royce Gruenler outlined when he stated, "We can expect to follow the same path of death and resurrection, despair, and peace."

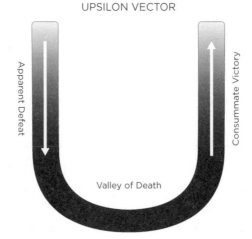

UPSILON VECTOR

Apparent Defeat

Consummate Victory

Valley of Death

Think of the upsilon's ironic pattern in nature as akin to the changing of the seasons, the kernel of wheat that falls to the ground and dies before it produces wheat, or great stories of antiquity such as when Persephone must first descend into the underworld and marry Hades before spring can be reborn. In Scripture, we see Jacob's hip dislocated before he undergoes his transformation into Israel (Gen. 32:22–32). All these examples help us remember the supreme example: our crucified Prince of Peace who rises from death so we "might walk in newness of life" (Rom. 6:4).

Unlike the "be happy and positive" approach to peacemaking found in much of popular Christianity, the New Testament vision is decidedly cruciform—it conforms to the cross of Jesus; it's sacrificial. This approach leads one to willingly sacrifice his or her privileges, comfort, pleasure, convenience, preferences, and personal agenda for the sake of peace. It's not surprised by other people's sin any more than Jesus is surprised by ours. In a fallen world it expects to encounter selfishness and strife, and when it does it responds with sacrificial mercy and grace. Like God who provided peace through the blood of Jesus's cross (Col. 1:20), we seek to extend peace in the same way—sacrificially.[14]

The Way of Peace

When we understand the integral connection between peacemaking and cross bearing, so much of the Sermon on the Mount comes into focus. For example, it illumines Jesus's words, "Do not resist the one who is evil. But if anyone slaps you on the right cheek, turn to him the other also" (Matt. 5:39). You might think of it as the "peace" created from a block of wood that sits between two metal objects to prevent the conduction of heat. In the words of minister Robert Henley, peacemakers are "'non-conductors' of bitterness, and wrath, and anger, and clamour, and evil-speaking, and all malice."[15]

In practical terms, our call to peacemaking is simply the public demonstration of what the Spirit is doing in our heart—the cultivation and showcasing of Christ at work. Eklund explains, "This beatitude has action written into it: blessed are the peace-*makers*, not [just] the peace-*filled*."[16] And, as Paul instructs his readers, "If possible, so far as it depends on you, live peaceably with all" (Rom. 12:18). Think of the virtues that comprise the Beatitudes: poverty of spirit, faithful mourning, meekness, hungering and thirsting for righteousness, mercy, and purity of heart. Such graces enable us to not simply encounter divine peace but also to share that peace with others.

A long tradition reaching back to the early church fathers suggests that the way to extend peace is by applying the preceding beatitudes.[17] For example, in contrast to the attachment to riches that characterizes so much of life in the West—the gluttony and greed that arouse anxiety and militate against peace—we need poverty of spirit. Amid our mourning, we need the empathetic tears and consolation of friends who share in our lament. In meekness we find the self-conscious renunciation of hostility that leads to shalom (Ps. 37:11). Hungering and thirsting for righteousness are crucial for peacemaking, as we considered earlier, for without a commitment to justice, peace becomes little more than a pious sentiment. And mercy is an essential accompaniment, without which we are liable to fall into bitterness and vengeance (Prov. 19:11). Last, there is purity of heart: when our hearts are renewed and purified by the God of peace (Col. 3:15).

The Urgency of Peace

An intern recently asked me, "What is the most significant obstacle to peace in the church today?" At once, a flurry of clanging conflicts came to mind: petty jealousies that spoil friendships, ambitions that disrupt unity and stultify the well-being of congregations, domestic strife that fractures marriages and results in divorce court. I thought of the distrust that sets elder councils against pastors and ministry staff against volunteers. In that fleeting moment, all of these and other acrimonious jangles occurred to me. But above them all emerged what might be the single greatest threat to peace in the contemporary church—political partisanship that prioritizes cultural values (many of them quite legitimate) over the Great Commission.

Today, many Christians correlate their political party with the manifest presence of Christ's kingdom and take a partisan posture that makes slogans and fits of outrage the chief ways they identify themselves. Consequently, members on the opposing side not only represent a different position but are viewed as a hideous evil that must be opposed. Such is the antagonism that now divides political progressives and political conservatives, even in the church.

Is it possible, however, for the church to approach this battle royale differently? Instead of suspicion and infighting, what if we expressed patience and kindness, enduring all things in the name of Christ (1 Cor. 13:4, 7)? What if we treated others the way we ourselves would like to be treated (Matt. 7:12; Luke 6:31)? What if we took Paul's words to heart, "Let your speech always be gracious, seasoned with salt, so that you may know how you ought to answer each person" (Col. 4:6) to heart?

Could we, for example, maintain a commitment to protecting the unborn and preserving God's design for the family while also addressing racial injustice and helping the poor? Our next chapter will consider how to pursue such a nonpartisan ethic in the name of Christ. For now, however, we simply want to consider the need for a posture that fears God and intentionally advances peace despite differences.

A chief reason for our failure to bring peace to these discussions, it seems to me, is overconfidence in our own intelligence coupled with a lack of respect for the other person. In his book *Humble Apologetics*, John Stackhouse helpfully elucidates the idea:

> To put it more sharply, we should sound like we really do respect the intelligence and spiritual interest and moral integrity of our neighbors. We should act as if we do see the very image of God in them. . . . It is a voice that speaks authentically out of Christian convictions about our own very real limitations and our neighbor's very real dignity, not cynical expediency. We are rhetorically humble because we are not prophets infallibly inspired by God, let alone the One who could speak "with authority" in a way no one else can speak. We are mere messengers of that One: messengers who earnestly mean well, but who forget this bit of the message or never really understood that bit; messengers who never entirely live up to their own good news; messengers who recognize the ambiguities in the world that make the message harder to believe; and therefore messengers who can sympathize with neighbors who aren't ready just yet to believe everything we're telling them.[18]

Don't misunderstand. This sort of peacemaking doesn't require us to compromise our theological convictions. It does, however, require us to emulate our crucified Savior, the one who demonstrated love toward enemies (Matt. 5:44). Jesus modeled such commitment throughout his life, but he especially did so on the cross. As John Stott puts it, "Nothing in history or in the universe cuts us down to size like the cross. All of us have inflated views of ourselves, especially in self-righteousness, until we have visited a place called Calvary. It is here, at the foot of the cross that we shrink to our true size."[19]

Instead of slouching into withdrawal (as cultural escapists) or charging into angry activism (to cancel our opponents), Christ calls his church to be like patient farmers who cultivate a harvest of righteousness "in peace by those who make peace" (James 3:18). This, according to F. W. Boreham, is the legacy of peacemakers:

> The spirit of peace wraps him about like an atmosphere; he exhales peace as a violet exhales sweetness; he breathes the very spirit of gentleness, geniality and goodwill. It is impossible to spend five minutes in his company without feeling the better for it. You rise from a meal with him feeling as if you were leaving a communion table. In the course of a walk with him, you remember the road to Emmaus. There is an unconscious influence about the true peacemaker that leads every man he meets to love his fellow-men.[20]

Perhaps you're thinking that such devotional language sounds too sweet and if I knew the level of antagonism you face among family and friends, I'd know how unrealistic it is. Fair enough. None of us are inherently able to embody peace amid difficult circumstances. That's why, from start to finish, it's God's gift, which he extends to us, in us, and through us. Jesus says, "Peace I leave with you; my peace I give to you. Not as the world gives do

I give to you. Let not your hearts be troubled, neither let them be afraid" (John 14:27). And to whom is this gift given? To children of God, for "his divine power has granted to us all things that pertain to life and godliness" (2 Pet. 1:3).

Our Identity as Sons of God

Jesus pronounces his blessing upon peacemakers, calling them "sons of God" (Matt. 5:9), not because peacemaking causes us to automatically *become* Christians. Rather, this blessing demonstrates that we *are* Christians, inhabited by the divine peacemaker, Jesus Christ. As Grant Macaskill puts it, "We are not simply saved *by* him, nor do we merely follow *after* him—though both of these continue to be true—but we participate *in* him."[21]

This is the meaning of the "sons of God" designation. From time immemorial, God's covenant people have been described with the language of "son" (Ex. 4:22–23), the ultimate declaration of which will come to the sight of the nations on the last day (Rev. 21:7–8). This acknowledgment, however, is not strictly in the future. God has already declared men and women in Christ to be his people on account of their union with him. In other words, because our truest self is now constituted by Jesus, we reflect his likeness (as a son resembles a father), a likeness that showcases divine peace. In the words of Leon Morris, "There is something godlike in bringing peace to people and people to peace."[22]

Our position as sons and daughters of God, therefore, leads us more and more into the divine practice of peacemaking. The pursuit of peace as a way of life, of course, doesn't come all at once, as anyone who has any experience in our world will ruefully attest. Peace is realized over time, little by little. As

Peter writes, Christ's righteous ones "seek peace and pursue it" (1 Pet. 3:11).

Like our heavenly Father whose redemptive peace plan reaches back to the dawn of creation, our peacemaking unfolds incrementally, working through this world's conflict and strife. The Creator's peace, after all, began in the Garden of Eden, was proclaimed through the centuries by Jewish prophets, and was ultimately fulfilled in the atoning death and resurrection of his Son, Jesus Christ. Such peace doesn't come easily or cheaply, but the God of peace, who raised our Lord Jesus from the dead, will surely cause it to prevail (Heb. 13:20).

"Blessed are the peacemakers, for they shall be called sons of God" (Matt. 5:9).

Even So, Rejoice

*Blessed are those who are persecuted for righteousness'
sake, for theirs is the kingdom of heaven. Blessed are you
when others revile you and persecute you and utter all
kinds of evil against you falsely on my account. Rejoice
and be glad, for your reward is great in heaven, for so
they persecuted the prophets who were before you.*

MATTHEW 5:10–12

CELIO SECONDO CURIONE, an Italian humanist whose heart was ignited by the writings of Martin Luther, was arrested by church authorities in 1523 for discussing Bible doctrine. Curione was summarily confined to a convent, where the inquisitor urged him to reconsider his newfound evangelical faith. Instead, he continued to read the Reformers, sharing their message of unmerited grace with anyone who would listen. In fact, he became so animated by Scripture that he eventually removed the bones from a saint's reliquary and replaced them with a copy of the Bible and the following caption: "This is the Ark of the Covenant where we find the true oracles of God; these are the true relics."[1]

This story illustrates the essence of Jesus's final beatitudes. Captured by the wonder of the gospel, Curione willingly endured persecution and reprisal, recognizing that Christ's kingdom was more compelling than personal safety or approval. It is a world-denying passion that reaches back to Moses. As the writer of Hebrews said,

> By faith Moses, when he was grown up, refused to be called the son of Pharaoh's daughter, choosing rather to be mistreated with the people of God than to enjoy the fleeting pleasures of sin. He considered the reproach of Christ greater wealth than the treasures of Egypt, for he was looking to the reward. (Heb. 11:24–26)

Perhaps you've noticed that the eighth and ninth beatitudes are different from what precedes. Up to this point, Jesus has emphasized the counterintuitive qualities of his Father's kingdom, the turn toward poverty of spirit that mourns over sin and expresses itself in meekness. He has described the soul that thirsts for divine justice and then extends that justice to others. A heart brimming with mercy, purity, and peace.

By contrast, however, the final two beatitudes describe the *outcome* of such a life—what happens when we manifest the purposes of Jesus on earth as they are in heaven. That unfortunate outcome, sooner or later, is persecution. As the apostle Paul noted, likely from personal experience, "Indeed, all who desire to live a godly life in Christ Jesus will be persecuted" (2 Tim. 3:12).

Living a Good Life

The pursuit of the good life is a universal human aspiration that reaches back to antiquity. Writing in the fourth century BC, Aristotle set forth his understanding of human flourishing as a life of virtue that accords with reason.[2] For Aristotle, such flourishing was realized within the city-state—a community that promotes justice and peace for all people.

The New Testament also envisions a community of justice and peace. However, the realization of such a community is not to be conceived as solely a human enterprise, an achievement that one acquires through discipline, philosophical reflection, or virtue formation. Rather, it is understood as something we enjoy by participating in Christ. From start to finish such participation (which makes someone a Christian) consists in divine peace and justice, precisely because our identity is defined by the person of Jesus. We are, as Grant Macaskill puts it, "contained in Christ's self and inhabited by his Spirit and [therefore] able to testify quite truly that we are children of God."[3]

This identification with Jesus, however, comes with a price. Through "many tribulations we must enter the kingdom of God" (Acts 14:22). The City of Man, we quickly discover, urges Christ-followers to avoid hardships for Jesus and embrace worldly blessedness instead. We are told, "Blessed are you when you succeed." This is hardly a new phenomenon. From the church's earliest days, Christians have been offered this Faustian bargain—to simply offer a pinch of incense to Caesar or admit that the Nazarene was simply one god among many and not the Lord of all.

Such evidence of this reality goes all the way back to the beginning. Cain killed his brother Abel "because his own deeds were evil and his brother's righteous" (1 John 3:12). Joseph was persecuted by his brothers and by Potiphar. Moses was nearly stoned by his countrymen. David was hunted down by Saul. Daniel was placed in a lions' den, John the Baptist was beheaded, and Jesus was scourged and crucified.[4]

While the news of most Christian martyrs today is known only to their friends and families, the challenges continue unabated, both large and small. As with previous ages, persecution ultimately lies not in certain forms of government or in unique historical factors. It lies in the unredeemed hostility of the human heart toward God (Rom. 8:7). The darkness hates the light and always will. Jesus said, "Remember the word that I said to you: 'A servant is not greater than his master.' If they persecuted me, they will also persecute you" (John 15:20).

And, tragically, when tempted to betray Christ in favor of worldly comfort and approval, the church has sometimes caved. It is not for us to judge, but to inspect our own hearts. Thankfully, that's not the end of the story. History testifies to the empowering grace of God that has enabled the church to persevere despite worldly pressure. Acts 4:19–20 reports that Peter and John once said, "Whether it is right in the sight of God to listen to you rather than to God, you must judge, for we cannot but speak of what we have seen and heard." Yes, persecution came, but so did gospel flourishing. As a result, the church "turned the world upside down" (Acts 17:6).

So, what does such a life in Christ look like in action? We can do no better than to look at the example of the apostle Paul.

Following the Suffering Servant

While the promise of divine peace is the heritage of every believer in Jesus, so too is the requirement that we, like him, carry a cross. We observe both of these callings—the peace of Christ and the persecution of Christ—in the ministry of Paul.

Down by a river in Philippi, Paul shared the liberating message of peace with a dealer in purple named Lydia. Day after day the apostle and his companions in gospel ministry explained the good news of the long-awaited Messiah and ruler of the kingdom of God, and their message was bearing fruit in this pagan region. Then the kingdom of darkness attempted to cast a shadow over everything.

A possessed slave girl described as an oracle showed up and began to cry out, "These men are servants of the Most High God, who proclaim to you the way of salvation" (Acts 16:17). The endorsement, similar to the attestations of demons during the earthly ministry of our Lord, was neither needed nor wanted. The Spirit would do his mighty work of salvation without any help from Satan's minions. Eventually, Paul responded to the situation.

"I command you in the name of Jesus Christ," the apostle said sternly, "to come out of her" (Acts 16:18). Immediately the shouting stopped, the girl returned to her right mind, and the demonic influence was gone. The girl's owners, however, were enraged. Their slave had made them a lot of money as a fortune teller, and now their retirement plan was ruined.

Quickly they stirred up the crowd and dragged Paul and Silas before the magistrates, accusing them of disturbing the peace and teaching unlawful customs. Without a trial, Paul and Silas were stripped, thrown at the whipping posts, and beaten with rods. The abuse was illegal, as both men were Roman citizens. Bruised and bloody, they were then thrown in a prison hole, where they were chained to the wall and left to suffer as night closed in.

I imagine it was when the blood was oozing out of their wounds and beginning to congeal that joy in their Savior began to escape their lips (Acts 16:25). Persecution was followed by hymns of praise, followed by peace. As if in answer to their spontaneous worship service, God showed up in power. An earthquake shook the prison and, as Charles Wesley would later write, their chains fell off and their hearts were free.[5] Deliverance had come!

Like Jesus, we can expect the same spiritual trajectory—down, then up. Too often we expect to have peace without persecution, glory without agony. But if we desire the one, we must expect to receive the other. This is only fitting. We deserve not peace and prosperity but pain and persecution, for we are the ones who pinned the Savior to the cursed tree:

No, it was not the Jews who crucified,
Nor who betrayed you in the judgment place,
Nor who, Lord Jesus, spat into your face,
Nor who with buffets struck you as you died.
No, it was not the soldiers fisted bold
Who lifted up the hammer and the nail,
Or raised the cursed cross on Calvary's hill,
Or, gambling, tossed the dice to win your robe.
I am the one, O Lord, who brought you there,
I am the heavy cross you had to bear,
I am the rope that bound you to the tree,

The whip, the nail, the hammer, and the spear,
The blood-stained crown of thorns you had to wear:
It was my sin, alas, it was for me.[6]

These words by Jacobus Revius (1586–1685) are the literary version of what his fellow countryman Rembrandt expressed when he painted himself at the foot of the cross. Like him, we are guilty. Like him, we deserve far more punishment than we have received. And like him, we identify with Christ, both in his resurrection and in his death.

A Countercultural Calling

You may have noticed the eighth and ninth beatitudes identify two reasons why persecution is considered blessed: when it is for righteousness' sake (Matt. 5:10) or when one is reviled and insulted for the name of Jesus (Matt. 5:11).[7] The latter is a reiteration and explication of the former—to accept the crown of thorns, slaps in the face, or mocking and jeering for following Christ. This is an important qualifier, for there is nothing virtuous about suffering for its own sake, especially when we have ourselves to blame. As Lloyd-Jones writes, "I suggest, therefore, that the most important thing to emphasize is this phrase, 'for righteousness' sake.'"[8]

In this cultural moment, we see plenty of ways that Christians bring suffering upon themselves. Those who spout hate or unbounded conspiracy theories invite derision or canceling on social media. Those who defend detestable or sinful behavior of their preferred politicians (on either side of the aisle) are rightly called hypocrites. Those who excuse breaches of integrity by saying the other side does worse are ridiculed as craven practitioners of whataboutism. In these and other cases, what such unrighteous acts and attitudes receive (and deserve) is justice.

At the same time, we must not deny that Christians today, even in the supposedly tolerant West, are being persecuted for the sake of righteousness. Those who refuse to participate in the active affirmation of unbiblical lifestyles so current in businesses and academies can find themselves ostracized, swept into court, or unemployed. Outside the West, Christians can face all kinds of dangers for refusing to deny their faith—or simply for the crime of identifying as followers of Christ. Fulani Muslim herdsmen in Nigeria, for example, murdered thirty-seven Christians over several weeks in the spring of 2022. Groups such as International Christian Concern are calling such persecution a genocide.[9]

This thicker account of the gospel recognizes that to be in Christ defines everything about us—every ambition, activity, purpose, and relationship—and this identity and calling will inevitably offend the sensibilities of the world. "Our citizenship is in heaven," says Paul, "and from it we await a Savior, the Lord Jesus Christ" (Phil. 3:20). While waiting, we discover that the shadowlands are inhospitable to the children of light. Put simply, the "kingdom" to which we belong "is not of this world" (John 18:36).

Because Jesus's kingdom is of another world, rabid partisanship is a problem for Christians. To be sure, the moral void of our day is corrosive and poses an ever-deepening threat to the common good of society. As embodied persons called to promote life and peace "on earth as it is in heaven" (Matt. 6:10), we should lament this corrosion, and, in the name of loving our neighbor, seek to promote righteousness. David Wells explains that "biblically speaking, it is entirely inappropriate for the church to become 'other-worldly'. . . . The church is clearly called to be thoroughly engaged with creation and with human life."[10] But, you may ask, how do we do that? Here is how the New Testament answers the question:

> Have this mind among yourselves, which is yours in Christ Jesus, who, though he was in the form of God, did not count equality with God a thing to be grasped, but emptied himself, by taking the form of a servant, being born in the likeness of men. And being found in human form, he humbled himself by becoming obedient to the point of death, even death on a cross. (Phil. 2:5–8)

Through centuries of reflection on this text, the church has agreed the self-emptying of Jesus reveals "the God of self-effacing, self-giving, self-sacrificing love."[11] Such is the heartbeat of Christ's kingdom. It is not another power structure that imposes itself on others, but humbly and self-consciously serves one's neighbor, even one's enemies. Thus, the kingdom advances not through cultural conquests or victorious elections but through patient service, warmhearted truthtelling, self-restraint, and turning the other cheek in the name of Christ.

Good News for the Persecuted

As mentioned, the ninth beatitude repeats and amplifies Jesus's words about persecution. By shifting from a third-person to a second-person address ("Blessed are *you*"), he zeroes in on his listeners—to the men and women surrounding him at the Sea of Galilee and those of us who would later read his words. This personalization conveys two important insights. First, Jesus correlates the kingdom with himself (those who persecute you "on my account," Matt. 5:11), clarifying that one's citizenship in God's community comes by following him. Second, he spells out the cost of discipleship—the reviling, persecution, and false accusations—that bears witness to his beatitudinal presence in action.[12]

Throughout his Gospel, Matthew underlines the persecution and defamation in store for Jesus's disciples. He presents Jesus's words to the Pharisees, such as, "Therefore I send you prophets and wise men and scribes, some of whom you will kill and crucify, and some you will flog in your synagogues and persecute from town to town" (Matt. 23:34)—a disappointing call for God's children, but one that reflects our King's own experience. Like Jesus, who interceded from the cross, "Father, forgive them, for they know not what they do" (Luke 23:34), disciples are called to pray for their persecutors: "But I say to you, Love your enemies and pray for those who persecute you" (Matt. 5:44). This is what citizenship in Christ's kingdom looks like—to drink the cup of suffering that our Lord Jesus drank (Matt. 20:23).

How then, you might wonder, is persecution good news, even to the point of producing joy? Simply put, it is the privilege of living for Christ's sake. It is the joy of now embracing by faith the ultimate reward that is promised in the kingdom of heaven.[13] This, after all, was the hope of the prophets "who were before you" (Matt. 5:12), the heralds who spoke for God amid opposition. Their situations differed greatly but as one godly company (note the plural), these prophets bore witness to the calling of Christ's disciples. To share in this glorious company is a privilege of such proportions that it rightly causes the Christian to rejoice.

Sadly, though, it's a joy that remains foreign to most of the world. The non-Christian attempts to dispel from his mind the reality of God and his kingdom. "That is the whole meaning of the pleasure mania of today," writes Lloyd-Jones early in the twentieth century (just imagine what he would say today about our day and age).[14] It's a commitment to live in the moment, in the immanent frame, where there's no talk about death, eternity, or judgment. And this approach is accelerating the deterioration of contemporary Christianity, turning it into a consumerist faith that is fueled by spiritual sugar rushes. As H. Richard Niebuhr memorably put it, it is like "A God without wrath brought men without sin into a Kingdom without judgment through the ministrations of a Christ without a Cross."[15]

Not so for disciples of Christ. Like Abraham, they look "forward to the city that has foundations, whose designer and builder is God" (Heb. 11:10). Full of hope, they can almost taste the final victory, like the prophets and saints of old who "all died in faith, not having received the things promised, but having seen them and greeted them from afar" (Heb. 11:13). Professor Wells describes the transforming power of this promise: "It is pointing beyond itself to that great day. It lives in this world, but it lives because it has seen the glory of the coming of the Lord. This is the knowledge that changes everything."[16]

Christianity and Martyrdom

Dietrich Bonhoeffer famously said, "When Christ calls a man, he bids him come, and to die."[17] Such Christianity regards suffering and persecution as a badge of true discipleship, for the cross of Jesus is the shape and substance of our identity. It is not the mark of super-Christians, inspiring heroes whose stories echo through the centuries. It is simply the proof of genuine faith. You might title it, "Christianity as Martyrdom."

The word "martyr," which means "one who bears witness," illustrates the missional impulse of this vision: disciples who pursue gospel witness as a matter of first importance, even at the expense of their lives. One thinks of stalwarts such as Jim Elliot, Pete Fleming, Nate Saint, Ed McCully, and Roger Youderian in Ecuador; Stephen and the apostles in the early church; Polycarp, a disciple of the apostle John who refused to offer incense to the emperor; Perpetua, who died in the arena; John Wycliffe, the fourteenth-century Bible translator of England; and Shahbaz Bhatti, a twenty-first-century Pakistani. These are a few of the uncountable multitude of Christian witnesses turned into martyrs over the centuries.

Just before the ascension, Jesus told his followers, "You will *be* my witnesses in Jerusalem and in all Judea and Samaria, and to the end of the earth" (Acts 1:8). We do not simply *do witnessing* as one ministry option among many, but we *are witnesses*, as a function of our identity. In other words, just as Jesus, the light of the world, advanced the kingdom wherever he went, so we, children of light, do the same. Because this witness emerges from the core of our being, it is most satisfying to our soul, even amid persecution.

Corrie ten Boom exemplified this quality of joy, a flowering of faith that grew out of her devotion to Christ. Imprisoned during World War II with her sister Betsie for hiding Jews, Corrie learned of the presence of God in her darkest hours. Her preparation for such a calling didn't happen overnight, but only after decades of purposeful and faithful living. In his book *Victorious: Corrie ten Boom and "The Hiding Place,"* Stan Guthrie describes God's painstaking preparation of this modern saint:

> In *The Hiding Place,* we see Corrie being prepared unknowingly in the little things of life for persecution and all that would come afterward. As Corrie noted later, "A person doesn't spring into existence at the age of fifty; there are years of preparation, years of experience, which God uses in ways we may never know until we meet Him face to face." We see this preparation in her long talks with Father about trusting the Lord and giving to him our deepest hurts. We see it in her ministry to children and the disabled—those little esteemed in the world, who could not pay her back. We see it in her decision to love and protect Jewish people in defiance of the Nazi regime. We see it in her care for other prisoners and for Betsie. We see it in her decision to forgive those who had hurt her. We see it in her decision to show the love of Jesus the Victor to those whose lives had been torn apart by war, even those who had collaborated. We see it in her decision to persevere through every obstacle.[18]

Such witnessing cannot be divorced from true kingdom faith. God calls some of us to be martyrs—witnesses for our faith—by laying down our lives. He calls others, perhaps in greater numbers, to be witnesses in the normal rhythms of life. Either way, "if we live, we live to the Lord, and if we die, we die to the Lord. So then, whether we live or whether we die, we are the Lord's" (Rom. 14:8). The reward will indeed be great.

Yet, disciples don't rejoice in suffering itself. Persecution, reviling, and false accusations, rather, are a crucial element in the process of participating in Christ, what Joel Lawrence has termed "death together."[19] Mindful of the kingdom's ironic turn (think upsilon vector), Lawrence explains the way toward becoming "the church for others," a concept of great significance in Dietrich Bonhoeffer's *Life Together*.[20] In Bonhoeffer's words, "The church is only church when it is there for others."[21] It's no coincidence that the final beatitude is followed by Jesus's metaphor about salt and light:

> You are the salt of the earth, but if salt has lost its taste, how shall its saltiness be restored? It is no longer good for anything except to be thrown out and trampled under people's feet. You are the light of the world. A city set on a hill cannot be hidden. Nor do people light a lamp and put it under a basket, but on a stand, and it gives light to all in the house. In the same way, let your light shine before others, so that they may see your good works and give glory to your Father who is in heaven. (Matt. 5:13–16)

After calling us to rejoice amid persecution, the Lord gives us an incentive to keep on going, no matter how the world may react. The vocation of bearing witness to the King of kings will have an outsized influence on a world that is lost in minuscule pursuits of security, success, and happiness. Our good works will be seen. Our Father will be glorified. So, we must let our light shine before others.

The Presence of the Kingdom

Sinners like us, despite our sincere desire to serve Christ, have an innate tendency to self-centeredness and are therefore unable to consistently fulfill our calling. In view of this problem, Bonhoeffer presents Jesus as "the human being for others," the Savior who liberates men and women from our idolatry to self.[22] It is precisely this freedom that enables us to look beyond ourselves to serve the needs of others. This enterprise of saying "no" to sin and manifesting "death together" is the tangible, embodied way of showing the world that Jesus Christ is Lord.

Bonhoeffer's life was devoted to this vision: to see the church function as the redemptive embodiment of Christ on earth. As we considered at the outset of this book, this vision was the impetus for the seminary he started for the Confessing Church at Finkenwalde, a program that was intentionally modeled after the Sermon on the Mount. To equip the church to stand against the onslaught of Nazism, Bonhoeffer put the Beatitudes squarely before his students.

It's worth noting that some people thought Bonhoeffer was going to an unhelpful extreme. Karl Barth, the famous Swiss theologian, was one. He accused Bonhoeffer, his friend and younger colleague, of creating "a seminary with an 'odour of a monastic eros and pathos.'"[23] To him, it seemed a bit Roman Catholic. Bonhoeffer, however, respectfully disagreed, contending that there is nothing wrong with prayer and rigorous study.[24]

Bonhoeffer's work *Life Together* was written to summarize the experiment of Finkenwalde and the principles by which the Confessing Church went deep with Christ, almost like a Christian boot-camp. Why was it like this? Because it needed to withstand the bitter persecution that lay ahead (for which God was preparing them). For such Christian formation there was no better curriculum than the Sermon on the Mount, with the Beatitudes at the leading edge. Jim Belcher explains:

[They] stressed the disciplines of holding one's tongue, meekness, listening, helpfulness, and bearing. One of the hardest disciplines at the seminary was the rule never to speak about a brother in his absence. Gossip was not allowed and talking behind someone's back was prohibited. . . . They were even required to have a prayer partner to whom to confess their sins, further teaching them how to die to themselves.[25]

In this way, Finkenwalde was not a retreat, a pietistic detour, or an exercise in legalism, as Barth suggested. It was a serious attempt at curbing sin and rising to fulfill the church's calling. This, it turns out, would be the opportunity before Bonhoeffer after he was arrested and placed in a gestapo prison. There, in that frightening darkness, the radiant community of Finkenwalde—rooted in the gospel—bore heavenly fruit.

Sigismund Payne Best, an English prisoner who shared a cell near Bonhoeffer at the Flossenbürg concentration camp, later described him as "all humanity and sweetness; he always seemed to me to diffuse an atmosphere of happiness, or joy in every smallest event in life, and of a deep gratitude for the mere fact that he was alive. . . . He was one of the very few men that I have ever met to whom God was real and ever close to him."[26] Best continued, "[His] soul really shone in the dark desperation of our prison. . . . [He] had always been afraid that he would not be strong enough to stand such a test but now he knew there was nothing in life of which one need ever be afraid."[27]

Bonhoeffer was ready. The Finkenwalde experience had instilled the requisite courage and faith to see Christ through the encircling darkness. Anticipating the eternal smile of Jesus himself, he was prepared to follow his Savior, "who for the joy that was set before him endured the cross, despising the shame, and is seated at the right hand of the throne of God" (Heb. 12:2). Here's how it went.

Less than twenty-four hours before he left this world, Bonhoeffer led a worship service among his fellow prisoners in the Schönberg schoolroom that was their cell. He read Isaiah 53:5, "With his stripes we are healed" and 1 Peter 1:3, "Blessed be the God and Father of our Lord Jesus Christ! By his great mercy we have been born anew to a living hope through the resurrection of Jesus Christ from the dead" (RSV). According to Best, Bonhoeffer "spoke to us in a manner which reached the hearts of all, finding just the right words to express the spirit of our imprisonment and the thoughts and resolutions which it had brought."[28]

Best continued,

He had hardly finished his last prayer when the door opened and two evil-looking men in civilian clothes came in and said: "Prisoner Bonhoeffer. Get ready to come with us." Those words "Come with us"—had come to mean one thing only—the scaffold. We bade him good-bye—he drew me aside—"This is the end," he said, "For me the beginning of life."[29]

The account of Bonhoeffer's final moments come from the camp doctor at Flossenbürg, H. Fischer-Hüllstrung. At the time he was unaware of Bonhoeffer's significance, but years later, he gave the following account:

On the morning of that day between five and six o'clock the prisoners . . . were taken from their cells, and the verdicts of the court martial read out to them. Through the half-open door in one room of the huts, I saw Pastor Bonhoeffer, before taking off his prison garb, kneeling on the floor praying fervently to his God. I was most deeply moved by the way this lovable man prayed, so devout and so certain that God heard his prayer. At the place of execution, he again said a short prayer and then climbed the steps to the gallows, brave and composed. His death ensued after a few seconds. In the almost fifty years that I worked as a doctor, I have hardly ever seen a man die so entirely submissive to the will of God.[30]

"Blessed are those who are persecuted for righteousness' sake, for theirs is the kingdom of heaven" (Matt. 5:10).

Epilogue

When Down Is Up

DURING MY FATHER'S first voyage across the Atlantic Ocean as a midshipman on the *USS Holland*, gray swells, some eighty feet from crest to trough, rolled in upon him. With each successive nosedive, daylight was eclipsed by encircling water, confronting the sailors with what appeared to be hell itself. Then, in a matter of seconds, the ship's bow would ascend toward heaven, causing the propeller (the "screw," in navy talk) to echo through the hull as the stern then ascended above the water. So the frightening undulation went, hour after hour. But that was not the worst part. Days earlier, Jeane Dixon, the famous psychic, had predicted that the *Holland* would sink on this voyage. Dixon's prophecy, like the churning storm, gripped the hearts of the anxious crew with each successive plunge.

Sometimes our Christian life is like the rolling motion of the *Holland*. Circumstances lift us heavenward, creating a sense of joy, before we find ourselves unexpectedly plummeting into a trough of despair. With each descent, the slanderous aspersions of the evil one fill our ears. "You are going to die." "God has forgotten you." "It's your fault." It is here that we know we should most vigorously pray for God's kingdom to come to us "on earth as it is in heaven" (Matt. 6:10). Some days, however, we lack sufficient strength and faith to reach out to God. Other days we can hardly say it with a straight face, aware as we are of our heart's rebellion and sin. But nonetheless we pray, recognizing that our crucified and risen Savior is alive, ready to comfort and strengthen us.

This undulating movement—from strength to weakness, from life to death—is enough to make us crazy (or at least queasy), that is, unless we see it as belonging to the larger pattern of God's counterintuitive kingdom. The Beatitudes, like few portions of Scripture, shine a spotlight on this pattern. Through weakness we manifest divine strength. Through poverty we find true wealth. Through apparent defeat we taste consummate victory.

The Beatitudes, in other words, are the Magna Carta of God's new world, the charter and commission of Christ's kingdom. They invite poor sinners like you and me to experience the new creation: to rest in his comfort, to embody his holiness, to savor his righteousness, to celebrate his mercy, to be called beloved children. This is the kingdom we are invited to, a kingdom that will last forever and ever.

How about you, my friend—how will you respond to the Beatitudes? Do you see them as a condemning set of spiritual requirements that you will never attain? As pious platitudes that will fail you in the so-called "real world"? As possibilities only when you have reached heaven, at the end of the journey?

Or do you take them as the Lord intends, to be an invitation, right now, to experience the King and his kingdom? Not so much a destination but a journey, despite the inevitable ups and downs, of increasing glory? Not so much a reward but your unfolding birthright as a son or daughter of God?

If so, you are truly blessed, for yours is the kingdom of heaven.

Notes

Introduction: You Are Invited

1. Throughout this book, I have included quotations from my own experience. Quotations without specific cited sources are in this category.

2. Aleksandr Solzhenitsyn, *The Gulag Archipelago* (New York: Harper-Collins, 1974), 168.

3. Cornelius Plantinga Jr., *Not the Way It's Supposed to Be: A Breviary of Sin* (Grand Rapids, MI: Eerdmans, 1995), 10.

4. For Dietrich Bonhoeffer, this culture clash is indeed strong, for it distinguishes the kingdom of God from the kingdom of this world. Dietrich Bonhoeffer, *The Cost of Discipleship* (New York: Touchstone, 2018), 108.

5. Servais Pinckaers, *The Pursuit of Happiness—God's Way: Living the Beatitudes*, trans. Mary Thomas Noble (Eugene, OR: Wipf and Stock, 2011), 36.

6. This study considers Matthew's version of the Beatitudes instead of Luke's abbreviated account largely because Matthew's is longer and more comprehensive. It also has a particular resonance with this contemporary moment, inasmuch as he stresses the ethical dimension of the kingdom, by presenting a vision of the Christian life that seeks to avoid cheap grace. Frederick Dale Bruner, *Matthew: A Commentary* (Grand Rapids, MI: Eerdmans, 2004), 1:172.

7. Jonathan T. Pennington, *The Sermon on the Mount and Human Flourishing: A Theological Commentary* (Grand Rapids, MI: Baker, 2017), 41.

8. Erasmo Leiva-Merikakis, *Fire of Mercy, Heart of the Word: Meditations on the Gospel According to Saint Matthew* (San Francisco: Ignatius, 1996), 183–84. This gloss is also upheld by Jonathan T. Pennington. According to Leiva-Merikakis, the ancient Greeks considered the gods to be fortunate "since they were immortal and hence free from the sorrow of our mortal life" (184). They were thought to possess a quality of wealth, power, and freedom that many ancients dreamed of. To obtain these advantages was to be considered *makarios*—blessed and fortunate, reflecting the perceived glory of pagan deities. Christ, however, turns the whole project on its head.

9. Augustine's work is titled *Of the Morals of the Catholic Church* (Savage, MN: Lighthouse, 2017), 21. Following a similar line of thought, Carl Henry helpfully explains how the "ethic of Eden and the ethic of Sinai and the ethic of the Mount of Beatitudes" hang together as one ethic. Carl F. Henry, *Christian Personal Ethics* (Grand Rapids, MI: Eerdmans, 1957), 290.

10. "Education: New Prospects, Old Values: Commencement Orators Offer Words to Live, Work and Pay Bills By," *Time*, June 17, 1985, http://content.time.com/.

11. Robert Schuller, *The Be (Happy) Attitudes: Eight Positive Attitudes That Can Transform Your Life* (Toronto: Bantam Books, 1987).

12. Schuller, *Be (Happy) Attitudes*, 8, 45.

13. The Confessing Church was a movement of Christians who resisted Hitler's attempt to unify Protestantism into a single, pro-Nazi church.

14. Craig J. Slane, *Bonhoeffer as Martyr: Social Responsibility and Modern Christian Commitment* (Grand Rapids, MI: Brazos, 2004), 239.

15. Bonhoeffer, *Cost of Discipleship*, 113–14.

Chapter 1: The Poverty That Makes One Rich

1. I have changed the name of this friend.

2. Leon Morris, *The Gospel according to Matthew*, The Pillar New Testament Commentary (Grand Rapids, MI: Eerdmans, 1992), 95.

3. John Nolland, *The Gospel of Matthew: A Commentary on the Greek Text*, New International Greek Testament Commentary (Grand Rapids, MI: Eerdmans, 2005), 200–201.

4. Jesus's Beatitudes are also found in Luke 6:20–26. For a comparison of these Gospel accounts see Rebekah Eklund, *The Beatitudes through the Ages* (Grand Rapids, MI: Eerdmans, 2021), 12–16.

5. Jonathan T. Pennington, *The Sermon on the Mount and Human Flourishing: A Theological Commentary* (Grand Rapids, MI: Baker, 2017) 101.

6. R. T. France suggests that the kingdom is a virtual "slogan for the whole scope of the ministry of Jesus." R. T. France, *The Gospel According to Matthew: An Introduction and Commentary*, Tyndale New Testament Commentaries (Leicester, UK: Inter-Varsity, 1985), 262.

7. Gene Edward Veith, *A Place to Stand: The Word of God in the Life of Martin Luther* (Nashville, TN: Cumberland House, 2005), 137.

8. Martin Luther, *The Freedom of a Christian*, ed. Timothy Wengert (Minneapolis: Fortress, 2016), 501.

9. Luther, *Freedom of the Christian*, 495.

10. Billy Graham Evangelistic Association, March 19, 2015, https://www.facebook.com/BillyGrahamEvangelisticAssociation/.

11. Jonathan Edwards, *The Works of Jonathan Edwards*, ed. Harry S. Stout and Nathan O. Hatch (New Haven, CT: Yale University Press, 2003), 22:290.

12. Robert Harris, *The Way to True Happiness: Delivered in Twenty-Four Sermons upon the Beatitudes*, ed. Don Kistler (Morgan, PA: Soli Deo Gloria, 1998), 28–29.

13. Thomas Watson puts it this way: "Here is the conduit of the Gospel, running wine to cherish such as are poor in spirit. . . . Here is the rich cabinet wherein the Pearl of Blessedness is locked up. Here is the golden pot in which is that manna which will feed and . . . revive the soul unto ever-lasting life. Here is a way chalked out to the Holy of Holies." Thomas Watson, *The Beatitudes: An Exposition of Matthew 5:1-10* (Carlisle, PA: Banner of Truth, 1971), 5.

14. Barna Group, "38 Percent of U.S. Pastors Have Thought about Quitting Full-Time Ministry in the Past Year," November 16, 2021, https://www.barna.com/.

Chapter 2: When Loss Becomes Gain

1. This opening story is adapted from my chapter, "The Resting Place" in *Lost and Found: How Jesus Helped Us Discover Our True Selves*, ed.

Collin Hansen (Deerfield: Gospel Coalition, 2019), 85–86. Used by permission.

2. Nicholas Wolterstorff, *Lament for a Son* (Grand Rapids, MI: Eerdmans, 1987), 89.

3. St. Augustine, *The City of God* (New York: Doubleday, 1958), 391–425.

4. J. I. Packer, *A Quest for Godliness: The Puritan Vision of the Christian Life* (Wheaton, IL: Crossway, 1990), 14.

5. Cornelius Plantinga, Jr., *Reading for Preaching: The Preacher in Conversation with Storytellers, Biographers, Poets, and Journalists* (Grand Rapids, MI: Eerdmans, 2013), 114.

6. Martyn Lloyd-Jones, *Studies in the Sermon on the Mount* (Grand Rapids, MI: Eerdmans, 1976), 44.

7. In the late eighteenth century, four out of five people died before reaching their seventieth birthday. Gary Laderman, *The Sacred Remains: American Attitudes toward Death 1799–1883* (New Haven, CT: Yale University Press, 1996), 24.

8. Nancy Guthrie, *Even Better Than Eden: Nine Ways the Bible's Story Changes Everything about Your Story* (Wheaton, IL: Crossway, 2018), 17.

9. Kelly M. Kapic, *Embodied Hope: A Theological Meditation on Pain and Suffering* (Downers Grove, IL: InterVarsity, 2017), 37.

10. Kapic, *Embodied Hope*, 38.

11. Jerry Root and Stan Guthrie, *The Sacrament of Evangelism* (Chicago: Moody, 2010), 152.

12. The author of this prayer is unknown but it seems it was first recorded in John Cotton, *The New-England Primer* (London: 1781).

13. This reflection on death first appeared in my article, "Pursuing Life Through (Christ's) Death," *Moody Alumni & Friends*, June 9, 2021, http://moody.edu. Used by permission.

14. Jonathan Edwards, *The Works of Jonathan Edwards*, ed. George S. Claghorn (New Haven, CT: Yale University Press, 1998), 16:753.

15. Jewish rabbis through the centuries have also rooted the blessing in Genesis 6:3, where it says, "Then the LORD said, 'My Spirit shall not abide in man forever, for he is flesh: his days shall be 120 years.'"

16. Handel composed the score for the oratorio in a mere twenty-four days, from August 22 to September 14, 1741. Since it was introduced in Dublin in 1742, there has not been a year in which it hasn't been performed, and it has been performed many times in most years.

Daniel I. Block, "Handel's Messiah: Biblical and Theological Perspectives," *Didaskalia* 12, no. 2 (Spring 2001): 1.

17. Block, "Handel's Messiah," 3.

18. J. Todd Billings, *The End of the Christian Life: How Embracing Our Mortality Frees Us to Truly Live* (Grand Rapids, MI: Brazos, 2020), 21.

19. George F. Handel, *Messiah* (Hong Kong: Naxos Digital Services, 2007).

20. Mark Talbot, *Give Me Understanding That I May Live: Situating Our Suffering within God's Redemptive Plan* (Wheaton, IL: Crossway, 2022), 125.

21. Talbot, *Give Me Understanding*, 125.

Chapter 3: Gentleness in a Hostile World

1. A. H. M. Jones, *Constantine and the Conversion of Europe* (Toronto: University of Toronto Press, 1978), 72.

2. Bryan Litfin, "Eusebius on Constantine: Truth and Hagiography at the Milvian Bridge," *Journal of the Evangelical Theological Society* 55 (2012): 775. Litfin examines the historical veracity of the Constantine story.

3. Earle E. Cairns, *Christianity Through the Centuries: A History of the Christian Church* (Grand Rapids, MI: Zondervan, 1996), 213.

4. John Calvin, *Commentary on a Harmony of the Gospels Matthew, Mark, and Luke*, vol. 1, ed. William Pringle (Grand Rapids, MI: Baker, 1998), 261–62.

5. Thomas Watson, *The Beatitudes: An Exposition of Matthew 5:1-10* (Carlisle, PA: Banner of Truth, 1971), 114.

6. Peter Kreeft, *Back to Virtue: Traditional Moral Wisdom for Modern Moral Confusion* (San Francisco: Ignatius, 1992), 140.

7. See David Briones, "Already, Not Yet: How to Live in the Last Days," Desiring God, August 4, 2020, https://www.desiringgod.org/.

8. George Eldon Ladd, *The Gospel of the Kingdom: Scriptural Studies in the Kingdom of God* (Grand Rapids, MI: Eerdmans, 1959), 40.

9. Martyn Lloyd-Jones, *Studies in the Sermon on the Mount* (Grand Rapids, MI: Eerdmans, 1976), 71.

10. Lloyd-Jones, *Sermon on the Mount*, 71.

11. Friedrich Wilhelm Nietzsche, *The Antichrist* (New York: Start, 2012), 62.

12. C. Ivan Spencer, *Tweetable Nietzsche: His Essential Ideas Revealed and Explained* (Grand Rapids, MI: Zondervan, 2016), 91.

13. Spencer, *Tweetable Nietzsche*, 91.
14. Darrell Sifford, "How Society Breeds the Passive Male," *Orlando Sentinel*, August 10, 1985, https://www.orlandosentinel.com/.
15. Sifford, "How Society Breeds the Passive Male."
16. The abusive males of Kristin Kobes Du Mez's narrative, particularly the militant heroes who have distinguished themselves by their "masculinity," are a shameful parody of Christian manhood. Du Mez, *Jesus and John Wayne: How White Evangelicals Corrupted a Faith and Fractured a Nation* (New York: Liveright, 2020).
17. Glenn T. Stanton, "The Problem With Men Today Isn't Toxic Masculinity, It's Passivity," *The Federalist*, September 11, 2018, https://thefederalist.com/.
18. Jordan B. Peterson, *Twelve Rules for Life: An Antidote to Chaos* (Toronto: Random House, 2018), 332.
19. Spencer, *Tweetable Nietzsche*, 97.
20. Servais Pinckaers, *The Pursuit of Happiness—God's Way: Living the Beatitudes*, trans. Mary Thomas Noble (Eugene, OR: Wipf and Stock, 2011), 62.
21. Fyodor Dostoyevsky, *The Brothers Karamazov* (New York: Barnes and Noble Books, 2004), 294.
22. For more on these blind spots, see Collin Hansen, *Blind Spots: Becoming a Courageous, Compassionate, and Commissioned Church* (Wheaton, IL: Crossway, 2015).
23. Cornelius Plantinga Jr., *Not the Way It's Supposed to Be: A Breviary of Sin* (Grand Rapids, MI: Eerdmans, 1995), 165–66.
24. Plantinga Jr., *Not the Way*, 166.
25. James Davison Hunter, *To Change the World: The Irony, Tragedy, and Possibility of Christianity in the Late Modern World* (New York: Oxford University Press, 2010), 107.
26. This statement was made in personal conversation in an interview I conducted with Lee Pfund for the Billy Graham Center.
27. This statement was made in personal conversation in an interview I conducted with Lee Pfund for the Billy Graham Center.

Chapter 4: Taste and See

1. This opening story was originally published in my chapter, "The Resting Place," in *Lost and Found: How Jesus Helped Us Discover Our*

True Selves, ed. Collin Hansen (Deerfield: Gospel Coalition, 2019), 84–95. Used by permission.

2. R. Kent Hughes, *Blessed Are the Born Again: The Beatitudes as a Checklist for Authentic Christianity* (Wheaton, IL: Victor Books, 1986), 45.

3. The seven deadly (or cardinal) sins are vices that engender other sins and further immoral behavior. First enumerated by Pope Gregory I (the Great) in the sixth century and further explicated in the thirteenth century by Thomas Aquinas, they are pride, greed, lust, envy, gluttony (including drunkenness), anger, and sloth.

4. As professor David Wells taught us in seminary, "Worldliness is anything in culture that makes sin look normal and makes righteousness look strange."

5. James K. A. Smith, *You Are What You Love: The Spiritual Power of Habit* (Grand Rapids, MI: Brazos, 2016), 57–81.

6. Smith, *You Are What You Love*, 58.

7. In Hebrew, Greek, and Latin, the words translated "righteousness" are also properly translated "justice." Either rendering is legitimate, though modern parlance often uses "righteousness" to convey personal behavior and employs "justice" to describe social action. Benno Przyblyski's meticulous study *Righteousness in Matthew and His World of Thought* helpfully elucidates the meaning and relative significance of *dikaiosynē* in Matthew, although I am not persuaded by his argument that it describes an ethical rightness in every occurrence. Benno Przyblyski, *Righteousness in Matthew and His World of Thought*, Society for New Testament Studies Monograph Series 41 (Cambridge: Cambridge University Press, 1980). Jonathan Pennington offers a clear and accessible summary of how the word is commonly understood in *The Sermon on the Mount and Human Flourishing: A Theological Commentary* (Grand Rapids, MI: Baker, 2017), 87–91. Donald A. Hagner convincingly unpacks the semantic range of the word beyond moral uprightness in "Law, Righteousness, and Discipleship in Matthew" in *Word and World* 18, no. 4 (Fall 1998): 364–71.

8. There is an ongoing debate over whether *dikaiosynē* in Matthew describes God's saving activity or the ethical behavior required of covenant members. Charles Lee Irons offers a careful survey and analysis of the debate in *The Righteousness of God: A Lexical Examination of*

the Covenant-Faithfulness Interpretation (Tübingen: Mohr Siebeck, 2015), 263–67. Many authors, however, understand Matthew to use *dikaiosynē* in both ways, depending on the context. My own interpretation affirms this idea. For example, Rebekah Eklund understands *dikaiosynē* to evoke the themes of social justice, moral development, and the status of human beings before God. Rebekah Eklund, *Beatitudes through the Ages* (Grand Rapids, MI: Eerdmans, 2021), 152. Jonathan T. Pennington similarly recognizes Matthew to use *dikaiosynē* "in relation to the Torah (5:21–28), righteousness in personal piety (6:1–21), and righteousness in relation to the world (6:19–7:11)." Jonathan T. Pennington, *Sermon on the Mount*, 89. Erasmo Leiva-Merikakis points out that *dikaiosynē* "generally implies a sense of right direction, of correct relationship—with the world, with other men, with God." Erasmo Leiva-Merikakis, *Fire of Mercy, Heart of the Word: Meditations on the Gospel According to Saint Matthew*, vol. 1 (San Francisco: Ignatius, 1996), 195. John Stott and Martyn Lloyd-Jones argue that *dikaiosynē* describes both a divine gift and behavior required of Christ's disciples. John R. W. Stott, *The Message of the Sermon on the Mount* (1978), 45; Martyn Lloyd-Jones, *Studies on the Sermon on the Mount* (Grand Rapids: Eerdmans, 1976), 64–67.

9. Stott, *Message of the Sermon on the Mount*, 44–47.

10. Flannery O'Connor, *Wise Blood: A Novel* (New York: Farrar, Straus, and Giroux, 1990), 22.

11. Augustine, *The Anti-Pelagian Writings*, ed. Philip Schaff, trans. Benjamin B. Warfield (Altenmünster: Jazzybee Verlag, 2017), 33.

12. Tony Lane, *Sin and Grace: Evangelical Soteriology in Historical Perspective* (London: Apollos, 2020), 21.

13. Cornelius Plantinga Jr., *Not the Way It's Supposed to Be: A Breviary of Sin* (Grand Rapids, MI: Eerdmans, 1995), 61.

14. "The bloodletting [bleeding] righteous; Rav Naḥman bar Yitzḥak says that this is one who lets blood by banging his head against the walls because he walks with his eyes shut, ostensibly out of modesty" (t. Soṭa 22b). Babylonian Talmud, The William Davidson Edition, http://www.sefaria.org/.

15. Tom Wright, *Simply Christian* (San Francisco: HarperSanFrancisco, 2006), 100.

16. G. K. Beale, *New Testament Theology: The Unfolding of the Old Testament in The New* (Grand Rapids, MI: Baker, 2011), 412–17.

17. "By his baptism Jesus affirms his determination to do his assigned work." D. A. Carson, *Matthew 1-12*, Expositers Bible Commentary (Grand Rapids, MI: Zondervan, 1995), 108. Pennington recognizes that in Matthew Jesus is the righteous one (27:19) who comes to bring about the consummation of righteousness. Pennington, *Sermon on the Mount*, 91.

18. Michael H. Crosby, *Spirituality of the Beatitudes: Matthew's Vision for the Church in an Unjust World* (Maryknoll: Orbis Books, 1981), 104–5.

19. Hagner writes, "Matthew is one with the other synoptic writers in stressing the coming of the kingdom in the person and ministry of Jesus." Hagner, "Law, Righteousness, and Discipleship," 368.

20. Hagner points out how the two go hand-in-hand: "The announcement of the dawning of the kingdom of God provides the larger framework within which the ethical demand is placed." Hagner, "Law, Righteousness, and Discipleship," 368.

21. Concerning this fulfillment in Jesus, Pennington writes, "It is indeed the true *teleios* form of righteousness that will result in [blessing]." Pennington, *Sermon on the Mount*, 89.

22. The righteousness in view here is an expression of the kingdom. Tugwell explains, "Surely the righteousness in question here can be connected with the righteousness of God's kingdom, which our Lord says should be the primary object of our seeking (Matt 6:33)." Simon Tugwell, *The Beatitudes: Soundings in Christian Tradition* (Springfield: Templegate, 1980), 75.

23. Hagner, "Law, Righteousness, and Discipleship," 368.

24. Augustus Toplady, "Rock of Ages, Cleft for Me" (1776).

25. Christiaan Mostert, "Justification and Eschatology," in *What Is Justification About? Reformed Contributions to an Ecumenical Theme*, ed. Michael Weinrich and John P. Burgess (Grand Rapids: Eerdmans, 2009), 187.

26. Mostert, "Justification and Eschatology," 187. While Matthew does not unpack the particulars of imputed righteousness, his construal of "righteousness" is grounded in a redemptive-historical fulfillment of the kingdom in the person of Jesus. Jonathan Pennington, *Sermon on the Mount*, 90. Irons, *Righteousness of God*, 265–66.

27. Victor Hugo, *Les Misérables: A New Unabridged Translation*, trans. Lee Fahnestock and Norman MacAfee (New York: Penguin, 1987), 76.

28. Hugo, *Les Misérables*, 103–4.

29. For more on this distinction, see Chris Castaldo, *Justified in Christ: The Doctrines of Peter Martyr Vermigli and John Henry Newman and Their Ecumenical Implications* (Eugene, OR: Pickwick, 2017), 168–87.

30. For an outline of this movement see Martyn Lloyd-Jones, *Studies in the Sermon on the Mount*, 82.

31. Leo Tolstoy, *Some Social Remedies: Socialism, Anarchy, Henry Georgism and the Land Question, Communism, Etc.* (Christchurch: Free Age, 1900), 29.

32. Leiva-Merikakis, *Fire of Mercy*, 195.

33. John Calvin, *Institutes of the Christian Religion*, ed. John T. McNeill, trans. Ford Lewis Battles (Louisville: Westminster John Knox, 1960), 1:798. Similarly, the Westminster Confession says, "Faith, thus receiving and resting on Christ and His righteousness, is the alone instrument of justification: yet is it not alone in the person justified, but is ever accompanied with all other saving graces, and is no dead faith, but works by love." Westminster Confession of Faith, "Of Justification" (Altenmünster: Jazzybee Verlag, 1881), 14.

34. For example, Jonathan Edwards strikes this note when he writes, "And one great thing [Jesus] aimed at in redemption, was to deliver them from their idols, and bring them to God." Jonathan Edwards, *The Works of Jonathan Edwards*, vol. 2 (1834; repr., Peabody: Hendrickson Publishers, 1998), 139.

35. Martin Luther, *Luther's Works*, ed. Jaroslav Pelikan (St. Louis: Concordia, 1956), 21:26.

36. Craig S. Keener, *A Commentary on the Gospel of Matthew* (Grand Rapids, MI: Eerdmans, 1999), 169–70. Similarly, Craig L. Blomberg argues that divine righteousness in the context of Matthew 5:6 denotes God's provision for the poor. Craig L. Blomberg, *Matthew: An Exegetical and Theological Exposition of Holy Scripture*, The New American Commentary Series (Nashville: B&H, 1992), 99–100.

37. R. T. France, *The Gospel According to Matthew: An Introduction and Commentary*, Tyndale New Testament Commentaries (Leicester, UK: Inter-Varsity, 1985), 94, 110.

38. Hughes, *Blessed Are the Born Again*, 47.

39. Bryan Litfin, "Eusebius on Constantine: Truth and Hagiography at the Milvian Bridge," *Journal of the Evangelical Theological Society* 55 (2012): 775.

40. "This covenantal justice is ultimately God's work of setting the world to rights," says Jonathan Pennington, "though we are [also] called to participate in this and are the beneficiaries of it." Pennington, *Sermon on the Mount*, 89.

41. It's the kind that George Orwell described in the slogan of *1984*: "War is peace. Freedom is slavery. Ignorance is strength." George Orwell, *1984* (New York: Signet Classics, 1977), 4.

42. Thaddeus J. Williams, *Confronting Injustice Without Compromising Truth: Twelve Questions Christians Should Ask About Social Justice* (Grand Rapids, MI: Zondervan, 2020), 1.

43. On this point I agree with John Stott, who refused to drive a wedge between gospel-focused discipleship and social justice and rather affirmed that the latter is the natural outworking of the former. Stott, *Message of the Sermon on the Mount*, 45.

44. Dietrich Bonhoeffer, *The Cost of Discipleship* (New York: Simeon and Schuster, 1995), 110.

45. David Wells waxes eloquent about such consumerism in *God in Wasteland: The Reality of Truth in a World of Fading Dreams* (Grand Rapids: Eerdmans, 1995), 49.

46. Martyn Lloyd-Jones, *Studies on the Sermon on the Mount*, 70.

Chapter 5: The Face of Mercy

1. Joseph Frank, *Dostoyevsky: A Writer in His Time* (Princeton: Princeton University Press, 2010), 176.

2. Frank, *Dostoyevsky*, 176–77.

3. Frank, *Dostoyevsky*, 177.

4. Frank, *Dostoyevsky*, 179.

5. Frank, *Dostoyevsky*, 180.

6. Frank, *Dostoyevsky*, 871.

7. Victor Hugo, *Les Misérables: A New Abridged Translation*, trans. Lee Fahnestock, Norman MacAfee, and Charles Edwin Wilbour (New York: Penguin, 1987), 170.

8. Bob Welch, *52 Little Lessons from Les Misérables* (Nashville: Thomas Nelson, 2014), 55.

9. Chris Abbott, *21 Speeches That Shaped Our World: The People and Ideas That Changed the Way We Think* (New York: Random House, 2010), 88.

10. Fantine says, "I have been a sinner, but when I have my child with me that will mean God has forgiven me." Hugo, *Les Misérables*, 200.

11. Hugo, *Les Misérables*, 189.

12. Hugo, *Les Misérables*, 197.

13. Rebekah Eklund, *The Beatitudes through the Ages* (Grand Rapids: Eerdmans, 2021), 175–76.

14. Eklund, *Beatitudes*, 176.

15. The fifth beatitude has a structure unlike any of the others in that the promised reward is identical to what God calls us to do.

16. Ewald M. Plass, *What Luther Says: An Anthology*, vol. 3 (St. Louis: Concordia, 1959), 1233–34.

17. Martin Luther, *Luther's Works*, ed. Jaroslav Pelikan (St. Louis: Concordia, 1956), 21:30. Calvin is likewise concerned with the practical dimensions of extending mercy: "We must assume their identity, as it were, so as to be deeply touched by their suffering and moved by love to mourn with them." John Calvin, *Sermons on the Beatitudes: Five Sermons from the Gospel Harmony, Delivered in Geneva in 1560* (Carlisle, PA: Banner of Truth, 2006), 42.

18. Plass, *What Luther Says*, 1233.

19. Eklund, *Beatitudes*, 192.

20. Martyn Lloyd-Jones, *Studies on the Sermon on the Mount* (Grand Rapids, MI: Eerdmans, 1976), 85–86.

21. Lloyd-Jones, *Sermon on the Mount*, 86.

22. John R. W. Stott, *The Message of the Sermon on the Mount* (Downers Grove, IL: InterVarsity, 1978), 29.

23. "Italian Woman Found Dead Seated at Table Found in Mummified State," *The Guardian*, February 8, 2022, https://www.theguardian.com/.

24. "Italian Woman Found Dead."

25. "Italian Woman Found Dead."

26. "Italian Woman Found Dead."

27. Rebekah Eklund explains the three basic ways the church has understood its calling to extend mercy: "helping the needy, forgiving the offender, and welcoming the outsider." Eklund, *Beatitudes*, 173.

28. John Calvin, *Sermons on the Beatitudes*, 42.

29. Jeremiah Burroughs, *The Saints' Happiness* (1867; repr., Soli Deo Gloria, 1992), 136.

30. Rabbis of the day taught their disciples that a righteous person forgives a transgressor only three times. D. A. Carson, *The Expositor's Bible Commentary: Matthew*, ed. Frank E. Gaebelein (Grand Rapids, MI: Zondervan, 1984), 405.

31. Simon Tugwell, *The Beatitudes: Soundings in Christian Tradition* (Springfield: Templegate, 1980), 93.

32. Corrie ten Boom, *The Hiding Place* (Grand Rapids, MI: Chosen, 2006), 247–48.

33. Sinclair Ferguson, *The Sermon on the Mount* (Carlisle, PA: Banner of Truth, 1988), 31.

34. I have changed the names of this couple.

Chapter 6: Seeing God

1. Edith L. Blumhofer, *Her Heart Can See: The Life and Hymns of Fanny J. Crosby* (Grand Rapids, MI: Eerdmans, 2005), 285.

2. Blumhofer, *Her Heart Can See*, 286. According to Edith Blumhofer, Manhattan was home to at least 121 evangelical city missions that featured "gospel meetings" (286).

3. Blumhofer, *Her Heart Can See*, 286.

4. Blumhofer, *Her Heart Can See*, 315.

5. According to H. Benedict Green, Matthew uses "heart" to describe a person's inner self, which includes volition and understanding. H. Benedict Green, *Matthew, Poet of the Beatitudes* (Sheffield: Sheffield Academic, 2001), 240.

6. This and the following paragraph have been adapted from my blog post, "Developing a Heart for God," July 22, 2021, chriscastaldo.com/.

7. John Bunyan, *Pilgrim's Progress* (Wheaton, IL: Crossway, 2009), 142.

8. James Black, *The Christian Life: An Exposition of Bunyan's Pilgrim's Progress*, vol. 2 (London: James Nesbitt, 1875), 182.

9. R. Kent Hughes, *Blessed Are the Born Again: The Beatitudes as a Checklist for Authentic Christianity* (Wheaton, IL: Victor Books, 1986), 66.

10. Matt Jenson, *The Gravity of Sin: Augustine, Luther and Barth on Homo Incurvatus In Se* (London: T&T Clark, 2006), 29. Drawing

on book fourteen of *The City of God*, Jenson examines the problems of isolation and conflict that emerge from the inward turn of sin, an egoism that is only healed when one turns from self to God.

11. Martin Luther, *Lecture on Romans,* ed. and trans. Wilhelm Pauck (Louisville: Westminster John Knox, 1961), 159.

12. Augustine, *City of God*, trans. Marcus Dodds (Edinburgh: T&T Clark, 1871), 26.

13. Augustine, *Confessions*, trans. Henry Chadwick (Oxford: Oxford University Press, 1991), 3.

14. J. Gary Millar, *Changed into His Likeness: A Biblical Theology of Transformation,* New Studies in Biblical Theology (Downers Grove, IL: InterVarsity, 2021), 174–77.

15. Portions of the following story have been adapted from my book *Holy Ground: Walking with Jesus as a Former Catholic* (Grand Rapids, MI: Zondervan, 2009). Used by permission.

16. John Newton, "Amazing Grace! (How Sweet the Sound)" (1779).

17. Erich Przywara, *An Augustine Synthesis* (Eugene, OR: Wipf and Stock, 2014), 494. There is, of course, more than a little of Plato's philosophical contemplation informing Augustine's conception of beatific vision. Nevertheless, the hope of one day seeing God remains a biblical notion that appropriately motivates the church.

18. An excellent treatment of the epistemological dimensions of the believer's encounter and vision of God is found in John Jefferson Davis, *Meditation and Communion with God: Contemplating Scripture in an Age of Distraction* (Downers Grove, IL: InterVarsity, 2012), 90–99.

19. Hughes, *Blessed Are the Born Again*, 64.

20. F. W. Boreham, *The Heavenly Octave: A Study of the Beatitudes* (London: Epworth, 1936), 114–15.

21. Boreham, *Heavenly Octave*, 114–15.

22. Luci Shaw, *Polishing the Petosky Stone: Selected Poems* (Vancouver: Regent College, 2003), 257–58. Used by permission of the author, Luci Shaw.

23. Joshua Schendel, "The Reformed Orthodox and the *Visio Dei,*" *The Reformed Theological Review* 77, no. 1 (April 2018): 27.

24. Michael H. Crosby, *Spirituality of the Beatitudes: Matthew's Vision for the Church in an Unjust World* (Maryknoll: Orbis Books, 2005), 143.

25. Philip D. Yancey, *What's So Amazing About Grace?* (Grand Rapids, MI: Zondervan, 1997), 198.

Chapter 7: Peace Be with You

1. Peacemaking is the final beatitude that believers are to pursue. It is distinguished from Jesus's concluding words of blessing, namely to those who are persecuted for righteousness' sake. Christians are not called to pursue persecution—certainly not in the way they're called to pursue the previous virtues (poverty of spirit, mourning over sin, meekness, hunger for righteousness, mercy, purity, and peace). But in this fallen world persecution is an unavoidable outcome of one's identification with Jesus.

2. Cornelius Plantinga Jr., *Not the Way It's Supposed to Be: A Breviary of Sin* (Grand Rapids, MI: Eerdmans, 1995), 9–10.

3. Scott McKnight, *Sermon on the Mount*, Story of God Bible Commentary (Grand Rapids, MI: Zondervan, 2013), 46.

4. Rebekah Eklund, *The Beatitudes through the Ages* (Grand Rapids, MI: Eerdmans, 2021), 237.

5. Eklund, *Beatitudes*, 240.

6. Craig L. Blomberg, *Matthew: An Exegetical and Theological Exposition of Holy Scripture*, The New American Commentary Series (Nashville: B&H, 1992), 100.

7. Thomas Watson, *The Beatitudes: An Exposition of Matthew 5:1-10* (Carlisle, PA: Banner of Truth, 1971), 209.

8. C. S. Lewis, *The Screwtape Letters* (San Francisco: HarperSanFrancisco, 2001), 25.

9. Todd E. Pressman, *Deconstructing Anxiety: The Journey from Fear to Fulfillment* (Lanham, MD: Rowman & Littlefield, 2019), 39.

10. Robert Schuller, *Be (Happy) Attitudes*, 191. In fairness to Schuller, he does affirm that "the only place you can get that kind of driving spirit, that kind of attitude, is from the Lord" (174). Unfortunately, this God-centered focus is obscured by his emphasis on "possibility thinking" (200).

11. Royce Gruenler of Gordon-Conwell Theological Seminary is the professor who I recall first using the phrase "upsilon vector." Part of this section has been adapted from my book *Holy Ground: Walking with Jesus as a Former Catholic* (Grand Rapids, MI: Zondervan), 2009. Used by permission.

12. The upsilon also looks like the letter *Y* when it's capitalized. Historians have called the upsilon Pythagoras's letter because the ancient

philosopher used it as a signpost on the path to virtue or vice. The Christian author Lactantius explained, "For they say that the course of human life resembles the letter *Y*, because every one of men, when he has reached the threshold of early youth, and has arrived at the place 'where the way divides itself into two parts,' is in doubt, and hesitates, and does not know to which side he should rather turn himself." Lactatius, *The Divine Institutes*, trans. William Fletcher, vol. 7 in *Ante-Nicene Fathers* (Buffalo: Christian Literature, 1886), bk. 4, chap. 3.

13. The following figure is taken from my book *Holy Ground*. Used by permission.

14. Martin Luther says it well: "He who is not a *crucianus*, so to speak, is not a *Christianus*: he who does not bear his cross is no Christian, for he is not like his Master, Christ." Ewald M. Plass, *What Luther Says: An Anthology*, vol. 1 (St. Louis, MO: Concordia, 1959), 357.

15. Robert Henley, *Saintliness: A Course of Sermons on the Beatitudes; Preached at St. Mary's Church* (London: Rivington, 1864), 80.

16. Eklund, *Beatitudes*, 239.

17. Eklund explains this history in her superb chapter on peacemaking: "For many premodern interpreters, one became peaceful by practicing all the previous beatitudes. For Ambrose, for example, the justice of the fourth beatitude leads naturally to the mercy of the fifth (since justice must be balanced with mercy, and merciful acts flow out of a desire to see justice done), and mercy requires purity of heart (the sixth) to be practiced rightly. Finally, purity of heart is needed for peacemaking." Eklund, *Beatitudes*, 239.

18. John G. Stackhouse, Jr., *Humble Apologetics: Defending the Faith Today* (Oxford: Oxford University Press, 2002), 229.

19. John Stott, *The Message of Galatians* (Downers Grove, IL: InterVarsity, 1968), 179.

20. F. W. Boreham, *The Heavenly Octave: A Study of the Beatitudes* (London: Epworth, 1936), 128.

21. Grant Macaskill, *Living in Union with Christ: Paul's Gospel and Christian Moral Identity* (Grand Rapids, MI: Baker, 2019), 2.

22. Leon Morris, *The Gospel according to Matthew*, The Pillar New Testament Commentary (Grand Rapids, MI: Eerdmans, 1992), 101.

Chapter 8: Even So, Rejoice

1. Salvatore Caponetto, *The Protestant Reformation in Sixteenth-century Italy*, trans. Anne Tedeschi and John A. Tedeschi (Kirksville, MO: Thomas Jefferson University Press, 1999), 42.

2. This is particularly observed in his *Nicomachean Ethics* and *Politics*. Dorothea Frede, "The Political Character of Aristotle's Ethics," in *The Cambridge Companion to Aristotle's Politics*, ed. Marguerite Deslauriers and Pierre Destrée (Cambridge: Cambridge University Press, 2013), 14–37.

3. Grant Macaskill, *Living in Union with Christ: Paul's Gospel and Christian Moral Identity* (Grand Rapids, MI: Baker Academic, 2019), 124.

4. Jeremiah Burroughs offers an impressive survey of the many biblical examples of God's people being persecuted by the world. Jeremiah Burroughs, *The Saints' Happiness* (1867; repr., Soli Deo Gloria, 1992), 205–6.

5. Charles Wesley, *And Can It Be, That I Should Gain?* (1738).

6. Leland Ryken, ed. *The Soul in Paraphrase: A Treasury of Classic Devotional Poems* (Wheaton, IL: Crossway, 2018), 111.

7. Rebekah Eklund, *The Beatitudes through the Ages* (Grand Rapids, MI: Eerdmans, 2021), 261.

8. Martyn Lloyd-Jones, *Studies in the Sermon on the Mount* (Grand Rapids, MI: Eerdmans, 1976), 111.

9. "Herdsmen Attacks Kill 37 Christians in Nigeria," *Evangelical Focus*, May 27, 2021, https://evangelicalfocus.com/.

10. David F. Wells, *God in the Wasteland: The Reality of Truth in a World of Fading Dreams* (Grand Rapids, MI: Eerdmans, 1994), 39.

11. David F. Wells, *The Courage to Be Protestant: Truth-Lovers, Marketers, and Emergents in the Postmodern World* (Grand Rapids, MI: Eerdmans, 2008), 194.

12. "Matthew," writes John Nolland, "is keeping 'persecuted' central, as one of the important links with v. 10, by placing it in the middle position." John Nolland, *The Gospel of Matthew: A Commentary on the Greek Text*, New International Greek Testament Commentary (Grand Rapids, MI; Eerdmans, 2005), 208–9.

13. Calvin writes that Jesus "reveals that if we cannot have our reward on earth, we should not lose heart, for our reward is in heaven."

John Calvin, *Sermons on the Beatitudes: Five Sermons from the Gospel Harmony Delivered in Geneva in 1560*, trans. Robert White (Carlisle, PA: Banner of Truth, 2006), 75.

14. Lloyd-Jones, *Sermon on the Mount*, 121.

15. H. Richard Niebuhr, *The Kingdom of God in America* (Middletown, CT: Wesleyan University Press, 1988), xv.

16. Wells, *The Courage to Be Protestant*, 248.

17. Dietrich Bonhoeffer, *The Cost of Discipleship* (New York: Touchstone, 1959), 89.

18. Stan Guthrie, *Victorious: Corrie ten Boom and "The Hiding Place"* (Brewster, MA: Paraclete, 2019), 111–12.

19. Joel D. Lawrence, "Death Together: Dietrich Bonhoeffer on Becoming the Church to Others," in *Bonhoeffer, Christ and Culture*, ed. Keith L. Johnson and Timothy Larsen (Nottingham: Apollos, 2013), 114.

20. Lawrence, "Death Together," 114.

21. Dietrich Bonhoeffer, *Dietrich Bonhoeffer Works*, ed. Gerhard Ludwig Müller, Albrecht Schönherr, Hans-Richard Reuter, Clifford J. Green, Geffrey B. Kelly (Minneapolis: Fortress, 1996), 8:503.

22. Bonhoeffer, *Dietrich Bonhoeffer Works*, 8:503.

23. Jim Belcher, "The Secret of Finkenwalde: Liturgical Treason" in *Bonhoeffer, Christ and Culture*, ed. Keith L. Johnson and Timothy Larsen (Nottingham: Apollos, 2013), 198. Dietrich Bonhoeffer, *Collected Works*, eds. Douglas W. Scott and Isabel Best (London: Collins, 1972), 2:121.

24. Belcher, "Secret of Finkenwalde," 198. Dietrich Bonhoeffer, *A Testament to Freedom: The Essential Writings of Dietrich Bonhoeffer* (San Francisco: HarperOne, 1995), 431.

25. Belcher, "Secret of Finkenwalde," 199.

26. Belcher, "Secret of Finkenwalde," 206.

27. Belcher, "Secret of Finkenwalde," 206.

28. Eric Metaxas, *Bonhoeffer: Pastor, Martyr, Prophet, Spy* (Nashville: Thomas Nelson, 2010), 528.

29. Metaxas, *Bonhoeffer*, 528.

30. Metaxas, *Bonhoeffer*, 532.

General Index

Scripture Index